dekalog

THE NEW HOME FOR SERIOUS FILM CRITICISM

The *Dekalog* series is a new list of bi-annual publications, released each March and September, dedicated to presenting serious and insightful criticism on a wide range of subjects across the full spectrum of contemporary global cinema.

Each issue is a guest-edited specially-themed volume including the writings of a diverse collection of authors, from academic scholars and cultural theorists, film and media critics, and filmmakers and producers, to various personalities involved in all kinds of institutionalised cinephilia such as film festival directors, cinema programmers and film museum curators.

The intention, therefore, is to include the multiple voices of informed and complementary commentators on all things cinematic in dedicated volumes on subjects of real critical interest, especially those not usually served by established periodicals or book-length publications.

In addition to specially commissioned essays, each issue also includes an exclusive '*Dekalog* Interview' with a leading figure related to the theme in question, and a '*Dekalog* Re-View' section where readers' feedback will be edited by respective guest editors and published in subsequent editions. All readers are therefore very much invited to participate in the discussions by contacting any of the series' guest editors on dekalog@wallflowerpress.co.uk

FORTHCOMING ISSUES IN THE *DEKALOG* SERIES:

Dekalog 2: On Manoel de Oliveira
guest edited by Carolin Overhoff Ferreira

Dekalog 3: On Film Festivals
guest edited by Richard Porton

Dekalog 4: On East Asian Filmmakers
guest edited by Kate Taylor

dekalog[1]
On The Five Obstructions

GUEST EDITOR: METTE HJORT

WALLFLOWER
LONDON & NEW YORK

First published in Great Britain in 2008 by
Wallflower Press
6 Market Place, London W1W 8AF
www.wallflowerpress.co.uk

A catalogue record for this book is available from the British Library.

ISBN 978-1-905674-75-6

Printed and bound in Poland; produced by Polskabook

Contents

Acknowledgements

Jørgen Leth responded promptly to various email enquiries, kindly spent time answering interview questions and provided helpful details concerning *The Five Obstructions'* festival appearances, awards and sales. He also kindly agreed to let us capture and print frames from *The Five Obstructions* and *Life in Denmark*.

I am grateful to audiences at the University of Wisconsin, Madison, at the University of Washington, Seattle, and at University College London for insightful discussions about *The Five Obstructions*, and to Yoram Allon at Wallflower Press for his enthusiasm for the project. Special thanks to Jacqueline Downs for her careful, patient and efficient editing.

Many thanks go to my colleagues and students at Lingnan University in Hong Kong, where even the briefest of encounters in the course of a busy day easily becomes a stimulating and memorable intellectual exchange.

The project was fully supported by a Direct Grant from Lingnan University (Project No. DR06B2), and I am very happy to acknowledge this financial assistance.

This book is dedicated to Edward Chen, president of Lingnan University 1995–2007, for having had the courage to pursue an extraordinary experiment, and the integrity and intelligence needed to make it a success.

Notes on Contributors

Susan Dwyer is Chair and Associate Professor of Philosophy at the University of Maryland, Baltimore County. Specialising in applied and theoretical ethics, her main area of research is moral psychology. Currently, she is working on a book entitled *The Normative Mind*. She is also the editor of *The Problem of Pornography* (Wadsworth Publishing, 1994) and (with Joel Feinberg) of *The Problem of Abortion* (Wadsworth Publishing, 1996), and the author of papers on reconciliation, free speech and feminist moral theory.

Mette Hjort is Professor and Programme Director of Visual Studies at Lingnan University. She has published *The Strategy of Letters* (Harvard University Press, 1993), *Small Nation, Global Cinema* (University of Minnesota Press, 2005) and *Stanley Kwan's 'Center Stage'* (Hong Kong University Press, 2006). She has also edited and co-edited a number of books, including *Rules and Conventions* (Johns Hopkins University Press, 1992), *Emotion and the Arts* (Oxford University Press, 1997), *Cinema and Nation* (Routledge, 2000), *The Postnational Self* (University of Minnesota Press, 2002), *Purity and Provocation: Dogma 95* (British Film Institute, 2003), and *The Cinema of Small Nations* (Edinburgh University Press, 2007). Her co-edited interview book entitled *The Danish Directors: Dialogues on a Contemporary National Cinema* appeared in English in 2001. She is currently working on a book focusing on film and risk.

Paisley Livingston is Chair Professor and Head of Philosophy at Ling-nan University in Hong Kong. His most recent book is *Art and Intention* (Clarendon Press, 2005), and he is currently co-editing, with Carl Plant-inga, *The Routledge Companion to Philosophy and Film*.

Trevor Ponech is Associate Professor of English, McGill University, Mon-tréal, and the author of *What Is Non-Fiction Cinema?* (Westview Press, 1999). His recent articles on the metaphysical and ontological assump-tions underlying contemporary philosophical and cognitivist film theories appear in the *Journal of Aesthetics and Art Criticism* and the *British Journal of Aesthetics*. He is currently at work on *Kitchen Stories*, a monograph on Bent Hamer's *Salmer fra kjøkkenet* ('Kitchen Stories', 2003) to be published in the University of Washington Press series, 'Nordic Film Classics'.

Hector Rodriguez is Associate Professor at the City University of Hong Kong. He is a cultural theorist and a digital artist. His animated video *Res Extensa* won the award for best work in the category of digital moving images in the 2003 Hong Kong Art Biennial. His game system *Coper-spective* was a finalist in the 'Graphics meets Games' competition of the Eurographics 2006 conference in Vienna. His work has been shown in Taiwan, India, China, Hong Kong, Austria and Germany. He is a mem-ber of the Writing Machine collective and has been Artistic Director of the Microwave Media Art Festival. His essays have been published in vari-ous film, media and game studies journals. Although his early writings were about Asian cinema and the philosophy of film, he now mainly writes about technological art and games.

Peter Schepelern is Associate Professor of Film and Media Studies at the University of Copenhagen. He has published books in Danish on film theory, Danish film history and on Lars von Trier. His publications in English include: 'Postwar Scandinavian Cinema', in *European Cinema* (Oxford University Press, 2003), '"Kill Your Darlings": Lars von Trier and the Origin of Dogma 95', in *Purity and Provocation: Dogma 95* (British Film Institute, 2003), 'The Making of an Auteur. Notes on the Auteur Theory and Lars von Trier', in *Visual Authorship: Creativity and Intention-*

ality in Media (Museum Tusculanum, 2005), 'Film According to Dogma: Ground Rules, Obstacles, and Liberations', in *Transnational Cinema in a Global North: Nordic Cinema in Transition* (Wayne State University Press, 2005) and 'Denmark', in *The Schirmer Encyclopaedia of Cinema* (Schirmer, 2006).

Murray Smith is Professor and Head of Film Studies at the University of Kent, Canterbury, where he has taught since 1992. Since 1995 he has been an advisory board member of the Society for Cognitive Studies of the Moving Image. His research interests include the psychology of film viewing, and especially the place of emotion in film reception; the philosophy of film, and of art more generally; music and sound design in film; and popular music. He is currently working on the implications of evolutionary theory for film culture. His publications include *Engaging Characters: Fiction, Emotion, and the Cinema* (Clarendon Press, 1995), *Film Theory and Philosophy* (co-edited with Richard Allen) (Clarendon Press, 1998), *Contemporary Hollywood Cinema* (co-edited with Steve Neale) (Routledge, 1998), *Trainspotting* (British Film Institute, 2002) and *Thinking Through Cinema* (co-edited with Tom Wartenberg) (Blackwell, 2006).

Preface

METTE HJORT

Released in 2003, Lars von Trier and Jørgen Leth's collaborative cinematic game and experiment, *The Five Obstructions* (*De fem benspænd*), has been received as one of the most intriguing and significant cinematic works of recent times. This unique film has prompted thoughtful reflection on a wide range of crucial issues and warrants careful and serious discussion. In providing an alternative to the format associated with various 'film classics' series, titles in the new *Dekalog* series allow for multi-faceted and multi-disciplinary engagements with particular issues and with significant films such as *The Five Obstructions*. The present volume therefore brings together a range of writers from diverse disciplinary as well as national backgrounds in an effort to begin the work of detailing and clarifying this important film's contributions to our understanding of the following issues: the role that other people play in facilitating self-understanding as an artist; creativity and its relation to constraint; the ways in which individual style can become a problem for artists; the role that play and collaboration assumes in creative processes; the effects of nesting works within works; and the relation between aesthetic and other sensibilities. The issue encompasses contributions by the following individuals: Susan Dwyer, an Australian ethicist residing in the US; Mette Hjort, a Danish film scholar living in Hong Kong; Hector Rodriguez, a Spanish philosopher, film scholar and award-winning digital artist; Paisley Livingston, a North American aesthetician and film scholar; Trevor Ponech, a Canadian film scholar; Peter Schepelern, one of Lars von Trier's former teachers at the University of Copenhagen; and Murray Smith, a US-trained British film theorist. Convinced at a deep personal level (and at first viewing) of the significance of von Trier and Leth's achievements with *The Five Obstructions*, the contributors generally approach the film from a perspective that reflects ongoing debates in their fields of expertise. The one exception to this rule is Schepelern, who was explicitly asked to discuss not so much the film itself but the controversy that erupted in 2005 when Leth published his memoirs, *The Imperfect Human* (*Det uperfekte menneske*). Leth's decision to publish this transgressive document cannot be ignored in the present context: the play on titles – *The Five Obstructions* comprises remakes of Leth's *The Perfect Human* (*Det perfekte menneske*, 1967) – makes it impossible to set aside the memoirs, and there can be little doubt that what some would consider the narcissistic exhibitionism of the latter text is related to Leth's sudden experience, as a result of *The Five Obstructions*, of a new level of success and international visibility. The persona described and articulated in this scandal-provoking document also has a bearing, whether we like it or not, on our assessment of Leth and his achievements with *The Five Obstructions*, for both are self-revelatory experiments on the boundaries of fiction and fact.

While it is often helpful in a preface to recapitulate the arguments presented in the various contributions, the aim in this case is rather different: to provide relevant (contextual) information that will further enhance viewers' experience of the film. Gathered here, then, is an email exchange between von Trier and Leth, in which the former outlines the project's basic conception and the latter accepts the proffered challenge; two manifesto-like statements in which the two directors formulate their preferred documentary aesthetics; a summary of the five obstructions with a brief gloss on each; excerpts from critical reviews of the film; a list of the film's festival appearances, prizes, and sales; and, finally, credits and other details pertaining to the film.

The origins of the project

The Five Obstructions, an 88-minute film and collaborative experiment involving Lars von Trier and Jørgen Leth (and co-financed by Yeslam bin Laden), can be traced back to a dinner party at documentary filmmaker Tómas Gislason's home in 2000. Von Trier was getting ready to launch Zentropa Real, a Zentropa subsidiary devoted to documentary filmmaking, and he invited Leth – his former teacher and mentor, and himself an accomplished filmmaker – to join him in marking the occasion with manifesto-like statements outlining their preferred documentary poetics. During the festivities von Trier suggested that he and Leth make a film together, and this led to the following email exchange between the two directors in November 2000:

Dear Jørgen,
The challenge/The Film you are supposed to solve/make is called: The five obstructions.

As a starting point I would like you to show me a 10-minute film, you have made – *The Perfect Human*.

We will watch the movie together and talk about it – then I will set up limitations, commands or prohibitions, which means you have to do the film all over again. This we will do five times – of this the title. I would find it natural if our conversations became a part of the final movie – with the six small films, of course.

I hope you're happy with the assignment. Maybe the subject for the first movie should be something we came to an agreement about? Of course we would have the most fun if the subject is of a character that gives us as big a difference as possible between film one and six?

Let me know how you feel about this. Please write.
Best regards,
Lars

Dear Lars,
I find the assignment tempting. I can see an interesting development between film one and six, the route around the obstacles, the conversations,

I'm sure we'll get a lot out of this. It is exciting. I look forward to your obstructions.

I really like the idea of having to change, adjust, and reduce according to given conditions in the process.

Best regards,

Jørgen

(reprinted in Danish Film Institute 2002: 31)

Directors' statements

As is often the case with von Trier, *The Five Obstructions* is associated with manifesto-like statements. While Leth, in the interview included in this volume, confesses to being unsure of the extent to which von Trier's concept of 'defocus' informed the actual making of *The Five Obstructions*, these statements from the year 2000 remain an important element of the project's original conception.

Defocus (von Trier)

We are searching for something between fiction and fact [often wrongly translated as 'something fictional, not factual']. Fiction is limited by our imagination and facts by our insight, and the part of the world that we are seeking cannot be encompassed by a 'story' or embraced from an 'angle'. The subject matter we seek is found in the same reality that inspires fiction-makers; the reality that journalists believe they are describing. But they cannot find this unusual subject matter because their techniques blind them. Nor do they want to find it, because the techniques have become the goal itself.

If one discovers or seeks a story, to say nothing of a point that communicates, then one suppresses it. By emphasising a simple pattern, genuine or artificial; by presenting the world with a picture puzzle with solutions chosen in advance.

The story, the point, the disclosure and the sensation have taken this subject matter from us – this; the rest of the world which is not nearly so easy to pass on, but which we cannot live without!

The story is the villain. The theme presented at the expense of all decency. But also the case in which a point's importance is presumably submitted for the audience to evaluate, assisted by viewpoints and facts counterbalanced by their antitheses. The worship of pattern, the one and only, at the expense of the subject matter from which it comes. How do we rediscover it, and how do we impart or describe it? The ultimate challenge of the future – to see without looking: to defocus! In a world where the media kneel before the altar of sharpness, draining life out of life in the process, the DEFOCUSISTS will be the communicators of our era – nothing more, nothing less!
Lars von Trier, March 2000 (ibid.)

The Moment Comes (Leth)

The part of a film I enjoy the most is when one can feel time flow through a single scene. There should always be room for time. A film should breathe naturally. When we go out, we set a trap for reality, so that we may persuade it to fit into that mindset we have organised. We are relaxed, attentive and noncommittal. Things happen when they happen. We are just as clever and just as stupid as fishermen. We can go out when we like in any defined direction and sometimes we stumble over a magic moment. That is what we are searching for, but we must not be too eager or too sure of it. Experience tells us that it exists. In our work, we are armed with our instinct, our eyes and our ears. We concentrate on empty space as well as occupied space. We observe silence and noise. We trust in chance's limitless gifts and yet the place in which we find ourselves isn't necessarily a product of chance. The moment suddenly comes when we are no longer astonished by its appearance. There we are. We are ready to capture it, to come to terms with it. We don't know where it will lead us. We follow the flow, we see where it wants to go and what it wants to do with us. We watch it take form and come together but we must ground it while it is still flowing and not too defined. We are in love. A feeling has bit us, we try to perceive it during its superficial passage yet are afraid of losing it again by understanding it too well.
Jørgen Leth, March 2000 (ibid.)

The five obstructions

In order to avoid repetitive descriptions of von Trier's obstructive rules in the articles that follow, these are summarised and briefly annotated here:

Obstruction #1: '12 frames; answers; Cuba; no set'

That is, Leth is to re-make *The Perfect Human* in Cuba, without using a set. No take can be longer than 12 frames and the questions posed in Leth's voice-over narration in the original film are to be answered.

Obstruction #2: 'The most miserable place; Don't show it; Jørgen Leth is the man; the meal'

Leth is to re-make *The Perfect Human* in the most miserable place that he can think of, but without actually showing the misery in question. He is himself to play the role played by Claus Nissen in the original film, and he is to focus on the sequence in which Nissen eats a gourmet meal.

Obstruction #3: 'Back to Bombay or Free-style film'

This either/or obstruction is imposed on Leth as a punishment for having failed to meet the requirements laid down in Obstruction #2. Given that Leth has clearly indicated that he cannot possibly return to Bombay, this obstruction effectively imposes a free-style film.

Obstruction #4: 'Animation'

Leth is required to re-make *The Perfect Human* as an animated film.

Obstruction #5: 'Lars von Trier will make the last obstruction. Jørgen Leth will be credited as director. Leth will read a text written by von Trier'

This particular obstruction is self-explanatory. The remakes resulting from the above obstructions are listed in *The Five Obstructions'* credits as follows:

The Perfect Human, Cuba, The Perfect Human, Bombay, The Perfect Human, Brussels, The Perfect Human, Cartoon, The Perfect Human, Avedøre, Denmark. In order to highlight the connection to the relevant obstructive rules, these films will be referred to in the discussions here as: *#1: Cuba, #2: Bombay, #3: Brussels, #4: Cartoon* and *#5: Avedøre.*

The film's reception

The Five Obstructions has over the past few years received glowing praise from critics and scholars alike. Here are some representative examples of what film critics have had to say about the film:

> 'Even if cinema is not exactly a competitive sport, part of the pleasure of the movie is watching von Trier meet his match.'
> – Mark Jenkins, *Washington Post*

> '*The Five Obstructions* succeeds on so many levels. The way in which Leth completes his task is frequently ingenious ... But the picture is perhaps most fascinating as a psychological portrait of two very different men ... This is your classic struggle between a great attack and a great defence.'
> – Xan Brooks, *Guardian Unlimited*

> 'The film is one of the most acute studies of the filmmaker/producer relationship since Godard's *Le Mépris*.'
> – Jonathan Romney, *Independent on Sunday*

> 'Though billed as a documentary, *The Five Obstructions* doesn't easily fall into any category. Perhaps it's best described as a game, in which a pair of Danish film directors from different generations spar with one another in a highly civilised, and surprisingly entertaining, fashion.'
> – David Stratton, *Variety*

> '*The Five Obstructions* clearly calls for a sequel, in which Leth would require von Trier to remake *Dogville*, despite Obstructions 6 through 10.'
> – Roger Ebert, *Chicago Sun-Times*

'A complete original. This ingenious, almost indescribable film won't re-
mind you of anything else because there is nothing else like it.'
  — Kenneth Turan, *Los Angeles Times*

'The next time you hear a director complain about the studio or his stars
or the weather or whatever, think of what Jorgen [sic] Leth achieved with
Lars von Trier as his boss — when five obstructions became five splendid
opportunities.'
  — Richard Corliss, *Time*

'Keep *Survivor* and *Fear Factor*, and give me this spellbinding mind teaser,
the ultimate game for movie buffs.'
  — Peter Travers, *Rolling Stone*

'The film is also valuable for raising awareness about Leth, whose work
hasn't been as widely recognised as that of his European contemporaries,
but who now makes an impressive case for his skills, five times over.'
  — Noel Murray, *The Onion*

Film festival appearances

The Five Obstructions has enjoyed considerable visibility on the international festival circuit, as the following list of appearances makes clear:

> Venezia Festival d'Arte Cinematografica, Italy (Aug. 27–Sept. 6, 2003)
> Toronto International Film Festival, Canada (Sept. 4–13, 2003)
> Malmö Nordisk Panorama, Sweden (Sept. 23–28, 2003)
> Rio de Janeiro Film Festival, Brazil (Sept. 25–Oct. 9, 2003)
> Sheffield Documentary Film Festival, Great Britain (Oct. 13–19, 2003)
> Bergen International Film Festival, Norway (Oct. 16–22, 2003)
> Valladolid International Film Festival, Spain (Oct. 24–Nov. 1, 2003)
> Lübeck, Nordische Filmtage, Germany (Oct. 30–Nov. 2, 2003)
> Sevilla Cinema and Sport Film Festival, Spain (Nov. 2–8, 2003)
> CPH Dox (Copenhagen Documentary Film Festival), Denmark
> (Nov. 7–16, 2003)

Esse&Bi Cinematografica, Italy (Nov. 10–15, 2003)

Gijon International Film Festival, Spain (Nov. 20–28, 2003)

Amsterdam, International Documentary Film Festival, The Netherlands (Nov. 20–30, 2003)

Mannheim-Heidelberg, International Film Festival, Germany (Nov. 20-29, 2003)

Oslo International Film Festival, Norway (Nov. 20–30, 2003)

Stavanger Sydvest Film AS, Norway (Nov. 21–23, 2003)

Tallinn Tarta, Black Nights Film Festival, Estonia (Nov. 22–Dec. 7, 2003)

Festival dei Popoli, Firenze, Italy (Nov. 28–Dec. 4, 2003)

Berlin European Film Academy Awards, Germany (Dec. 6, 2003)

Sundance Film Festival (Park City), USA (Jan. 15–31, 2004)

Prague Febiofest, International Film, TV and Video Festival, Czech Republic (Jan. 22–30, 2004)

Göteborg Film Festival, Sweden (Jan. 23–Feb. 2, 2004)

Laboratoire Éclair, France (Feb. 1, 2004)

Berlin–Royal Danish Embassy, Germany (Feb. 1–10, 2004)

Budapest Danish Film Week, Hungary (Feb. 10–25, 2004)

Stockholm Cinemateket, Svenska Filminstitutet, Sweden (Feb. 14–16, 2004)

New York Film Society of Lincoln Center, USA (Feb. 19, 2004)

Tampere Film Festival, Finland (Mar. 3–7, 2004)

Buenos Aires, Mar Del Plata International Film Festival, Argentina (Mar. 11–20, 2004)

Bermuda Film Festival, Bermuda (Mar. 19–25, 2004)

Den europæiske dokumentarfilmfestival, Norway (Mar. 29–Apr. 4, 2004)

Belgrade International Documentary & Short Film Festival, Serbia (Mar. 30–Apr. 04, 2004)

Montevideo International Film Festival of Uruguay, Uruguay (Apr. 3–18, 2004)

Hong Kong International Film Festival, China (Apr. 6–21, 2004)

Buenos Aires Festival Internacional de Cine Independiente, Argentina (Apr. 14–25, 2004)

Vilnius International Film Festival, Lithuania (Apr. 30–May 9, 2004)

Linz, Crossing Europe Film Festival, Austria (May 4–9, 2004)

Madrid, Documenta Madrid, Spain (May 7–12, 2004)

München Documentary Festival, Germany (May 7–15, 2004)

Sofia, Royal Danish Embassy, Bulgaria (May 28–Jun. 4, 2004)

Sydney Film Festival, Australia (Jun. 11–25, 2004)

Durban International Film Festival, South Africa (Jun. 14–27, 2004)

Helsinki Midnight Sun Film Festival, Finland (Jun. 16–20, 2004)

International Television and Film Festival Cologne, Germany (Jun. 17–23, 2004)

Vila Do Conde Festival Internacional de Curtas Metragens, Portugal (July 3–11, 2004)

Jerusalem International Film Festival, Israel (July 8–17, 2004)

Auckland International Film Festival, New Zealand (July 9–25, 2004)

Cape Town South African International Documentary Film Festival, South Africa (July 16–26, 2004)

Wellington, New Zealand Film Festival, New Zealand (July 16–Aug. 1, 2004)

Melbourne Film Festival, Australia (July 21–Aug. 8, 2004)

Warsaw, Era New Horizons Film Festival, Poland (July 22–Aug. 1, 2004)

Zagreb Motovun Film Festival, Croatia (July 26–30, 2004)

Brisbane International Film Festival, Australia (July 27–Aug. 8, 2004)

Odense International Film Festival, Denmark (Aug. 9–14, 2004)

Sarajevo Film Festival, Bosnia-Herzegovina (Aug. 20–28, 2004)

Athens International Film Festival, Greece (Sept. 10–19, 2004)

Helsinki Film Festival, Finland (Sept. 16–26, 2004)

Honningsvag, North Cape Film Festival, Germany (Sept. 16–19, 2004)

Riga Arsenals, Latvia (Sept. 18–26, 2004)

Valdivia International Film Festival, Chile (Sept. 25–Oct. 1, 2004)

Vancouver International Film Festival, Canada (Sept. 28–Oct. 8, 2004)

Academy Awards Foreign Language Film, USA (Oct. 1, 2004–Apr. 1, 2005)

Toronto Harbourfront Super Danish, Canada (Oct. 22–Nov. 5, 2004)

Lisbon International Documentary Film Festival, Portugal (Oct. 24–31, 2004)

Jihlava International Documentary Film Festival, Czech Republic (Oct. 26–31, 2004)

Aarhus Film Festival, Denmark (Oct. 27–31, 2004)

Maribor, DokMa, Slovenia (Nov. 2–6, 2004)

Tempo Dokumentarfilmfestival, Sweden (Nov. 11–14, 2004)
Reykjavik Film Festival, Iceland (Nov. 17–22, 2004)
Taipei Golden Horse Film Festival, Taiwan (Nov. 25–Dec. 5, 2004)
Suriname IDFA Flies T®opics, The Netherlands (Nov. 29–Dec. 5, 2004)
Mumbai International Film Festival, India (Jan. 6–13, 2005)
Mexico City International Contemporary Film Festival, Mexico
    (Feb. 16–27, 2005)
Adelaide International Film Festival, Australia (Feb. 18–Mar. 3, 2005)
ZagrebDox, Croatia (Feb. 22–26, 2005)
Sao Paulo It's All True International Documentary Film Festival, Brazil
    (Mar. 29–Apr. 10, 2005)
Moscow EU Film Festival, Russia (Apr. 13–26, 2005)
Singapore International Film Festival, Singapore (Apr. 15–30, 2005)
Jeonju International Film Festival, South Korea (Apr. 28–May 6, 2005)
Sponge Co., Ltd. Seoul EU Film Festival, North Korea (May 6–20,
    2005)
Tokyo, Hokuou Tanpen Festival, Japan (May 21–29, 2005)
Brasilia EU Film Festival, Brazil (Jun. 1–July 1, 2005)

Prizes awarded

The Five Obstructions has been nominated for a number of prestigious awards (including Best Documentary at the European Film Awards (2003)), and has to date won the following prizes:

Durban International Film Festival 2004: Best Documentary
Gulddok 2004: Gold Dok of the Year
Odense International Film Festival 2004: Grand Prix
Zagreb Motovun Film Festival 2004: FIPRESCI Jury Prize

Sales

International distribution is always a challenge for small-nation film-makers, and it is thus worth noting that *The Five Obstructions* has been sold to the USA, United Kingdom, France, Russia, Spain, Italy, Germany,

Switzerland, Austria, Belgium, The Netherlands, Luxembourg, the Czech Republic, Bulgaria, Poland, Ukraine, Moldovia, Hungary, the Slovak Republic, the Baltic States, Australia, New Zealand, Argentina, Chile, Mexico, Venezuela, Peru, Bolivia, Colombia, Uruguay, Panama, Nicaragua, Honduras, Belize, Haiti, the Dominican Republic, Israel, Turkey, Norway, Sweden and Finland.

Credits and other relevant details

Actors, in order of appearance:
Claus Nissen, Maiken Algren, Daniel Hernández Rodríguez, Jacqueline Arenal, Vivian Rosa, Jørgen Leth, Patrick Bauchau, Alexandra Vandernoot

Produced by Carsten Holst
Executive producers: Peter Aalbæk Jensen, Vibeke Windeløv
Co-executive co-producers, Marc-Henri Wajnberg, Morin, Nicole Mora

Director of photography: Dan Holmberg, DFF
Assistant director of photography: Adam Philp
Second unit director and photographer: Asger Leth
Sound design: Hans Møller ApS
Line producer: Marianne Christensen
Assistant producer: Signe Birket-Smith
Film editing: Camilla Skousen, Morten Højberg
First assistant director: Asger Leth
Assistant director: Asger Leth
Personal assistant to Lars von Trier: Thomas Schindel
Personal assistant to Carsten Holst: Nina Munch Petersen
Production assistants, Zentropa Real: Rasmus Christoffersen, Jordan Savel, Majken Bramstrup, Jesper Grüner

The Perfect Human, Cuba
Assistant line producer: Anders Jacobsen
Head of production: Magdalene Garcia
Production coordinator: Javier Gonzales

Sound engineer: Martin Saabye Andersen
Make-up: Magdalena Coamano
Production driver: José Luis Figueroa
Casting: Magdalena Garcia, Marianne Christensen
Voice-over: Jørgen Leth

The Perfect Human, Bombay
Head of production: Amrit Gangar
Production coordinators: Suhas Bhiwandkar, Floyd E. Casper, Deepak Rao
Sound engineer: Jan Juhler
Voice-over: Jørgen Leth

The Perfect Human, Brussels
Maid: Marie Dejaer
Body Double: Melanie Munt
Couple: Meschell & Pascal Perez
Delegate producer: Marc-Henri Wajnberg
Head of production: Tom Heene
Assistant producer: Marie-Aude Goddard
Wajnbrossse assistant producers: Mairead O'Leary, Rogier van Eck, Manka
Sierakowski, Isabelle Corlier
Second director of photography: Adam Philp
Assistant director of photography: Manuel Dacosse
Production coordinator: Johannne Stainer
Location manager: Delphine Coterel
Runner: Steffan Maenen
Sound engineer: Paul Heymans
Props: Michel Vinck/Amalgames
Stylist: Elisabeth Houtard/Amalgames
Make-up artist: Lisa Schonker
Hair stylist: Juan Pacifico
Sound equipment: Triangle 7
Lighting equipment: Ze Light
Insurance: Olivier Heger
Script: Jørgen Leth & Asger Leth

Poem, 'The Woman': Sophie Destin
Voice-over: Patrick Bauchau

The Perfect Human, Cartoon
Gangster: Bent Christensen
Naked man: Anders Hove
Naked woman: Charlotte Sieling
Man with jacket: Jan Nowicki
Woman with money: Stina Ekblad
Delegate producer: Marc-Henri Wajnberg
Animation director: Bob Sabiston
Animation: Randy Cole, Jennifer Drummond, Holly Fisher, Michael Layne,
Katy O'Connor, Bob Sabiston, Susan Sabiston, Patrick Thornton
Sound engineers: Tom Koester, Paul Heymans
Animation consultant: Asger Leth
Script: Jørgen Leth & Asger Leth
Voice-over: Jørgen Leth & Patrick Bauchau
Scenes from *Good and Evil, Notes on Love* and *Tropical Mix*, all by Jørgen Leth
Animation produced by Flat Black Films, Austin, Texas, USA

The Perfect Human, 1967
Director: Jørgen Leth
Woman: Maiken Algren
Man: Claus Nissen
Script: Ole John & Jørgen Leth
Cinematography: Ole John & Henning Camre
Music: Henning Christiansen
Film editing: Knud Hauge
Produced by Laterna Film

The Perfect Human, Avedøre, Denmark
Script: Lars von Trier
Voice-over: Jørgen Leth
Conversations: Director: Jørgen Leth; Obstructor: Lars von Trier
Directors of photography, 3rd unit: Jakob Bonfils & Kim Hattesen

Editing: Daniel A. Dencik
Sound engineers: Morten Bottzauw, Jens de Place Bjørn, Kasper Munck-
Hansen

Post-production
Post-production managers: Anne Katrine Andersen, Mette Høst Hansen
Post-production supervisor: Pia Nielsen
Assistant, post-production: Christine Ekstrand
Assitants, editing: Simon Kristiansen, Lasse Martinussen
Technical consultant: Lars Dela
Post-production facilities: Klippegangen ApS
On-line editors: Marlene Billie Andreasen, Simon Kristiansen
Digital colour grader: Thomas Therchilsen
Visual effects: Gearless ApS
Video to film transfer: Rekorder ApS, Thomas Caspersen
Post-production: Éclair Laboratoires, France, Véronique Durand, Cécile Piot,
Colour by Dejonghe
Filters: Fabien Pascal

Music consultants: Mikkel Maltha, Anders Valbro, Zentropa Music ApS

With support from Eurimages, Danish Film Institute (consultant, Jakob Høgel)

In co-production with DR TV, Memfis Film International, Centre du Cinéma
et de l'Audiovisuel de la Communauté Française de Belgique.
In collaboration with Nordic Film & TV Fund (Kristin Ulseth, Eva Færevaag
and Svend Abrahamsen), Swedish Film Institute (consultant, Göran Olsson),
SVT/Björn Arvas, YLE TV1 Co-productions, Channel 4, Canal+ Scandinavia,
Loterie Nationale

World Sales: Trust Film Sales 2 ApS, Wajnbrosse Productions, Almaz Film Productions

WORKS CITED

Brooks, Xan (2003) 'The Pupil's Revenge,' *Guardian Unlimited*, 7 November. Available at: http://film.guardian.co.uk/interview/interviewpages/0,,1080386,00.html (accessed 12 January 2005).

Corliss, Richard (2004) 'Five Difficult Pieces', *Time*, 30 May. Available at: http://www.ti.com/time/magazine/article/0,9171,1101040607-644160,00.html (accessed 12 January 2005).

Danish Film Institute (2002) *Film: Special Issue / Leth*. Copenhagen: Danish Film Institute.

Ebert, Roger (2004) *Chicago Sun-Times*, 10 September. Available at: http://rogerebert.suntimes.com/apps/pbcs.dll/article?AID=/20040910/REVIEWS/409100307/1023 (accessed 12 December 2005).

Jenkins, Mark (2004) 'Five Obstructions: Filmmaker Faceoff', *Washington Post,* 26 March. Available at: www.washingtonpost.com/wp-dyn/articles/A24183-2004Mar25.html (accessed 10 January 2005).

Murray, Noel (2004) *A.V. Club*, 25 May. Available at http://www.avclub.com/content/node/17762 (accessed 17 August 2007).

Romney, Jonathan (2003) 'Lars von Trier, nil; Jorgen [sic] Leth, five', *Independent on Sunday*, 9 November. Available at: http://film.guardian.co.uk/interview/interviewpages/0,,1080386,00.html (accessed 12 January 2005).

Stratton, David (2003) 'The Five Obstructions', *Variety*, 2 September. Available at: http://www.variety.com/review/VE1117921689.html?categoryid=31&cs=1 (accessed 1 February 2005).

Travers, Peter (2004) 'The Five Obstructions', *Rolling Stone*, 18 May. Available at: http://www.rollingstone.com/reviews/movie/6054636/review/6053991/the_five_obstructions (accessed 12 August 2007).

Turan, Kenneth (2004) 'The Five Obstructions', *Los Angeles Times*, 4 June. Available at: http://www.calendarlive.com/movies/reviews/cl-et-five4jun04,2,7450503.story (accessed 12 August 2007).

Romancing the Dane: Ethics and Observation

SUSAN DWYER

So far as we know, we are the only species capable of introspection, and thus, sometimes, of insight into our own individual and collective nature. Arguably, the entire discipline of philosophy and, much more recently, of psychology, is premised on this simply stated but complicated fact. We are also a social species, each of us desiring – perhaps, even needing – to live as one among others. Taken together, these perfectly trite observations invite a number of questions regarding the nature of the self and self-consciousness, and about the possibility of successful intersubjective communication. One line of enquiry among these questions, one that is vigorously pursued in *The Five Obstructions*, concerns the extent to which an individual's self-understanding depends on the availability to that person of a genuinely second-person perspective. In order properly to understand oneself, does one need to see oneself through another's eyes – in particular, the eyes of another who is in relation with us? If the answer is affirmative, what obligations do we have to each other to provide second-person perspectives? How is such a perspective to be achieved? How is it best achieved, morally speaking?

As I will try to show here, *The Five Obstructions* provides a very powerful example of self-revelation facilitated by another. Towards the end of the film, Lars von Trier remarks, 'There are just a few areas in life on which I think I'm an expert. One of them is Jørgen Leth. I think I know considerably more about him than he does. So this entire project has been a "Help Jørgen Leth" Project.' Such a pronouncement sounds insufferably arrogant. Still, von Trier does succeed in revealing Leth to himself and thereby to us. What makes for this success and, crucially, what renders that revelation morally less problematic than it might otherwise be, is that Leth himself collaborates in the revealing. Von Trier's obstructions, posed against the assumption of Leth's perfectionism, permit Leth to participate in an activity that clearly makes him happy (filmmaking) to learn about aspects of himself.

Moral risks can result from the typically asymmetrical relation between observed and observer. These are alluded to in the conversation von Trier and Leth have about Obstruction #2 – remaking *The Perfect Human* in the 'most miserable place on earth'. A central issue in the ethics of documentary filmmaking is the extent to which the subjects of such films are exploited. The filmmaker may be well-intentioned, may want to tell 'her story' truthfully, but it is the filmmaker who has ultimate control over what is represented and how it is represented. Power wholly or largely resides with the person directing the camera. And subjects, despite the fact that they are shown talking and acting, are wholly or largely passive in the production of the finished representation. The fact that some styles of filmmaking deploy various distancing techniques only underscores the worry that the filmmaker is merely 'using' her subjects. The filmmaker's task is not to be involved with her subjects, but objectively to represent them.[1] Leth admits, 'The observer is my role, of course. It's my instinct.' And von Trier wants Leth to test whether he (Leth) has any moral qualms about coolly observing the suffering of others. Von Trier: 'I want to move you on from there. To make you empathise. I'd like to send you to the most miserable place on earth … Can you think of any places, any themes one cannot exploit?' Can Leth engage in the privileged activity of remaking his own film in the midst of genuine human degradation and abjection without somehow being affected by that environment?

We shall return to the answer below. For the moment, it is worth remarking that *The Five Obstructions* brilliantly re-presents these questions about the moral significance of the asymmetry between observed and observer at the meta-level. After all, *The Five Obstructions* is a film about Leth remaking *The Perfect Human*. However, Leth is hardly passive in this enterprise. To be sure, he is subject to von Trier's constraints and he bridles against them. But Leth fully exercises his agency in responding to them. My point here is that the agentive participation of the observed in a *dialogue* of revelation immunises that process against the charge of moral exploitation and renders von Trier's assertion of epistemic authority about Leth less arrogant.[2]

And, of course, *The Five Obstructions* is about von Trier himself. At times, he is explicit about this. For example, when he describes his first obstruction (that edits cannot be longer than 12 frames) as 'vicious', von Trier seems to be confirming what some critics say about him as a director. He shows, that is, some measure of insight into how others see and judge him. And yet, the film also reveals much more about von Trier and his passions. In a wonderfully ironic twist, von Trier writes an account of what he may have revealed about himself as if it were penned by Leth. He has Leth read this account as a voice-over to the fifth remake.

In what follows, I shall briefly outline why there is value in being exposed to second-person perspectives on oneself. In addition, I shall mention some of the inherent difficulties in communicating such perspectives, and argue for the particular utility of filmic representation as a mode for such communication. Then I shall turn to discuss what I call the three movements of *The Five Obstructions*, meaning here to refer to (i) the representation of humankind in Leth's original 1967 film, *The Perfect Human*, (ii) the collaboratively produced representations of von Trier and Leth in the remakes under Obstructions #1 through #4, and (iii) those same representations in the remake under Obstruction #5. My intention here is simply to illustrate how filmic representations can indeed play a role in the task of grasping the second-person perspectives I claim are essential to sound self-understanding. At the end, I will offer some remarks about a larger theme that hovers around the activity of *The Five Obstructions*. This has to do with an old debate between romanticism and rationalism. In this film and in subsequent interviews about it, Leth remarks on what he takes to be von Trier's romanticism, that is, the latter's notion

Leth returns from Cuba exuberant rather than defeated

that only by immersing ourselves in the messiness and (perhaps) horror of human life can we honestly engage with it and with ourselves. Against this, Leth can be read as a cool rationalist. In the end, I think, we learn not that the romantics were wrong to insist on the possibility of self-creation. What we learn from this deeply affectionate cinematic *pas-de-deux*, is that self-creation requires more than a single self.

Self-understanding, second-person perspectives and representation

The human capacity – arguably unique among animals – to have thoughts about our thoughts or, as philosophers put it, to have second-order mental states, is both a blessing and a curse. Its upside is that it allows for self-reflection; its downside is that it allows for self-reflection. Still, while too much iterated thinking about one's beliefs and desires can lead to madness, some measure of self-understanding would seem to be essential for agency of any plausible kind. Commonsense alone tells us that planning, deliberation about action and cognitive change (revision) must involve an individual's being able to reflect and modify aspects of her psychology. Self-understanding, as I use the term, consists in a grasp of and an evaluative relation to a substantial subset of one's beliefs and desires, hopes and fears, traits and dispositions, habits and aspirations, and so on. Taken as a whole, self-understanding consists in a relatively veridical and stable self-conception. Its connection to the very possibility of agency, and hence its role in moral action, cannot be overestimated.

It is patently clear, however, that regarding self-consciousness and introspection, no person is infallible about themselves. There are complex theoretical reasons for this (articulated, for example, by Maurice Merleau-Ponty (1962)), and it is obvious that we are each vulnerable to various psychological and social biases. Not only do such biases work in various self-serving ways to distort our self-conceptions, they can also literally screen off certain kinds of first-person access to features of the self. Furthermore, the sorts of conceptual apparatus required in order to engage in serious reports to oneself about oneself are acquired in the course of normal human development: small children, arguably, lack self-understanding.

There is a rich philosophical history – especially, in the Continental tradition, and, as a result of feminist thinking, more recently in the Anglo-American tradition – concerning the central role that the social environment plays in the natural development of self-understanding. Paul Ricoeur (1966), for example, suggests that an individual's sense of being the originator of her actions depends on her being embedded among other individuals who can be literal witnesses of these actions. And relational views of autonomy are gaining ground (see, for example, Meyers 1989; Nedelsky 1989).[3]

The main points here are that (i) in the course of development, we need others even to acquire the capacities that make self-understanding possible, and (ii) throughout our lives, we need others as necessary correctives and 'completers' of our self-understandings. My claim is not that any individual's self-conception can be made accurate and complete by others; it is just that an individual cannot even approach such ideals without others.

But not just any others will do. As Ricoeur would say, we need to see ourselves reflected in others' eyes and that image must be trustworthy. Hence, we rely on those with whom we are in close relation – second-persons, not merely third-persons – to help show us to ourselves. Achieving genuine insight into oneself, I believe, requires ongoing non-exploitative opportunities to see oneself as strange (to oneself).

Now, of course, I cannot take up your perspective on the world. I can imagine it, I can empathise with your situation, but I can never really see and experience life as you do. My grasp of your understanding and experience of things will always be *mine*. We are, as it were, locked in our minds. And these barriers are as relevant to my grasp of your experience of me as they are to my grasp of your experience of eating ice-cream. A close friend can tell me things about myself I might otherwise not be able to know. But how much better if she can *show* me those things; if she can coax – *not* manipulate – out of me actions and behaviours that are genuinely revelatory of my self.

Lars von Trier has found one way to do this – for Jørgen Leth. My central claim is that *The Five Obstructions* can be read as a sustained exercise about what we can learn – perhaps, can *only* learn – from representations of ourselves produced by others. Von Trier succeeds, because Leth can trust the representation. It is co-produced, in a medium that is a common passion between them, and in the context of a palpably affectionate relationship.

The first movement: *The Perfect Human* (1967)

Leth's original short film, *The Perfect Human*, has been described as 'an elegant mock-anthropological treatise on man's imperfectability' (Corliss 2004: 23), and as 'a suave pseudo-scientific examination of human behavior' (Scott 2004: E5). 'Mock-' and 'pseudo-' are essential modifiers here, for the piece is surely ironic. Human beings are represented doing typically human things, but we are given no sense of how it is for them to do those things. It is as if they are mindless. Consider, for example, the hollow monologue Claus Nissen delivers during the dinner scene. One does not get the sense at all that this man is really inquiring into the fleetingness of joy; neither does he seem genuinely concerned for the loss of 'you' – whomever she may be. So, here is a perfectly unedifying – because so rabidly third-person – representation of humankind.

The second movement: Obstructions #1 through #4

Obstructions #1 through #4 gradually reveal Leth (*qua* filmmaker and *qua* person) as he responds cinematically to von Trier's obstructions. Just as Dogma 95's original Vow of Chastity lays out rules specifically designed to work against conventionalism, von Trier's obstructions are designed to force Leth out of his habits, those in his filmmaking as well as those of his self. They impose, in a way, the necessary critical distance for Leth to see himself more clearly. As such, *The Five Obstructions* reveals von Trier at his Brechtian best. It is not just that he (von Trier) makes Leth strange to himself, he has Leth create the very vehicles that manifest that strangeness.

Von Trier ferrets out precisely the constraints that Leth will find the most challenging. Only someone intimately familiar with Leth could have chosen these obstructions to such good effect. Von Trier is not, despite the frequent allusions (both in *The Five Obstructions* and reviews of the film) to punishment, humiliation, sadism, and so on, trying to punish Leth or trip him up in order to humiliate him. Von Trier is trying to get Leth to understand himself, to expose himself to himself. Consider, for example, the following exchange that takes place after Leth has returned with the film from the second obstruction. Von Trier complains that it is not the film that he asked for, that it did not capture what he thought mattered. Since Leth refuses to go back to Mumbai and remake the film, von Trier says he must be 'punished', but note the form the punishment takes – it is a direct appropriation of Leth's response.

> Von Trier: You've put me in a spot. We have not achieved what I wanted. So I have to punish you somehow. What should the punishment be?
> Leth: What should it be? It should fit the crime.
> Von Trier: Yes, but what kind of method should be applied?
> Leth: I can't say. I prefer you to make the decisions.
> Von Trier: So make a film with no rules from me.

And Leth does; showing that nothing is no obstacle to something.

I have argued above that successful, non-exploitative self-revelation facilitated by a second-person depends not just on familiarity between the observed and the observer, but also on trust. The remaking of *The Perfect Human* under the first, third and fourth obstructions are, morally speaking, perfectly unproblematic. It is not so clear that this is true of the remakes under the second and fifth obstructions. (Since I will directly address the latter in the next section, I will limit my immediate remarks to the former.)

A brief recapitulation of some dialogue will be helpful here:

Von Trier: The highly affected distance you maintain to the things you describe. That's what I want to get rid of in my next obstruction.

Leth: It's not merely a pose.

Von Trier: Not at all. But I want to put your ethics to the test. We talk so much about the ethics of the observer.

Leth: The observer is my role, of course. It's my instinct.

Von Trier: I want to move you on from there. To make you empathise. I'd like to send you to the most miserable place on earth … How far are you prepared to go if you are not describing something? Would anything rub off? I want you to go close to a few really harrowing things. Dramas from real life that you refrain from filming.

Leth chooses the red light district of Bombay (that is, Kamathipura, a district of what is now called Mumbai). Despite, or perhaps because of, its being India's banking capital and the home of the huge Indian film industry, Bollywood, Mumbai is home to some 12 million people, 8 million of whom live in slums. Falkland Road is the main thoroughfare, if that term can be used at all, through Kamathipura. Here is a recent description of the area:

The tiny lanes which slice the area into ribbons are packed with people and their belongings. While food is being prepared on a stove, a child defecates next to it. Somebody is having a bath a few feet away and yet somebody else is fornicating close by. In the midst of all this are hawkers, card sessions, goats on a tether, pimps on the prowl, customers looking for a bargain, tourists and countless sex workers. The air is thick with pollutants and decibel levels can rupture an uninitiated eardrum with ease. (Menen 2001)

Along it and in the alleys that snake around it live some 200,000 prostitutes. The sex trade operates on three levels. At the lowest ranks are the girls and women who literally live on the street; they will rent a room in one of the 'cages' that line the buildings on Falkland Road, in which the second tier of prostitutes live and work. Above the cages are brothels, several floors with narrow corridors lined with small rooms in which as many as three girls or women live and work. Children who are not yet sex workers themselves share this space night and day. American photographer Mary Ellen Mark describes a typical scene:

Falkland Road is lined with old wooden buildings. On the ground floor there are cage-like structures with girls inside them. Above the cages the buildings rise three or four storeys, and at every window there are more girls – combing their hair, sitting in clusters on the windowsills, beckoning potential customers. They vary in age from eleven-year-old prostitutes to sixty-five-year-old madams. (1981: 11)

It is indeed, as Leth says, a horror scene (see also Levine 2004). But why, we might ask, does Leth choose this place? After all, he is far more familiar with an arguably worse place, a place in which he lives for part of each year: Haiti. Still, the choice of either location as a mere backdrop, as a mere test of Leth's 'cool', raises moral questions. Despite the fact that Leth is shown smiling (hence, interacting?) with some denizens of the Falkland Road, this really is a case of human beings and their degradation being used merely to make some other point – namely, that Leth, as a matter of fact and in spite of his pre-Mumbai remarks to the contrary, *is* affected by their suffering.

It is somewhat troubling to discover that Leth is annoyed at having to admit this fact too. The conversation between von Trier and Leth is at its testiest after they have watched the Mumbai film:

> Von Trier: It was not the film I asked for.
>
> Leth: Well I'll be damned. Let's hear why not.
>
> Von Trier: One of the rules I asked for was that we shouldn't see those people.
>
> Leth: Yes, but I interpreted that loosely.[4]
>
> Von Trier: I have to say I disapprove. I'm going to have to send you back, you know.
>
> Leth: You can't.
>
> Von Trier: I'm afraid I'll have to. I'm afraid I have no option.
>
> Leth: It's a place I can't go back to.

Leth then explains exactly why:

> When I left here last time I was in shock. I thought, 'It's impossible! Yet another suicidal situation! It's too hard. I have no desire to do it. How can I find the desire?' It was really harsh of you. Even so, an idea came to me. I asked myself, 'Where are the most awful places I've seen?' The first place to occur to me was a horrific experience of the red light district, Bombay. I'd seen it a few years previously. I'd seen it six or seven years ago. I thought it a horror beyond compare. The kind of thing you run away from screaming. I am not afraid of prostitutes in general. But this was a picture from hell. We shot the film. I was cold-blooded and I had no scruples. I thought, 'Damn it, we can do this!' Then I had a night after that. Two nights. I had one of those rare nightmares you remember when you wake up. The analytical thought occurred to me that there was something Faust-like about it. A pact. Something diabolical, some kind of alchemy. By going to the limits you also pay the price of going to the point where fear transforms into madness, to put it bluntly. When you have to avoid sleep so as not to fall back into that nightmare, you're in deep shit.

So, yes, Leth learns something about himself. And that something might be unsettling to him. For either he learns that he is fully capable of exploiting the suffering of real persons in the service of what he himself says is just a 'game', or he learns that his view of himself as a sublimely cool observer is not in fact correct.

The third movement: Obstruction #5

As mentioned above, the film made under the fifth obstruction involves Leth reading (as a voice-over) a script written by von Trier that takes the form of a letter written from Leth to von Trier about the central conceit of *The Five Obstructions*. The letter is read over a montage of scenes from their earlier encounters and conversations, from the original *The Perfect Human*, and from the remakes.

That letter would seem flatly to contradict my main thesis. Here are some relevant pieces of the 'letter':

> You thought, 'Jørgen is trying to hide his true self – behind his provocative perverse perfection. He wants to conceal his angst behind a personal fiction of rows of Armani suits on hangers protecting him through his months of depression on Haiti' ... You ordered me around and issued prohibitions to distract me, to penetrate my armour ... But no matter how odd the clarinet sounded, you could not see behind my eyes. No matter how close you got, you couldn't see beneath the skin of my hand to the nerves and most delicate blood vessels. *Nothing was revealed* and nothing helped ... You say, I didn't dare find my way into what I so dishonestly and skilfully conceal and you imagine to be so valuable. But it's no good. The dishonest person was you, Lars. You only saw what you wanted to see ... But *you exposed yourself* ... This is how the perfect human falls. [Emphasis added]

But, as I indicated in the previous section, something of Leth *was* revealed. Still, von Trier/Leth is right to point out that second-person perspectives – like all perspectives – have their limitations. They too are subject to biases, psychological defences, wishful thinking and other distortions. Hence, insofar as we rely on others' views of us to develop our own self-understandings, we must be aware of what we know about those others' limitations. Perhaps there were certain antecedent hypotheses about Leth's character that von Trier intentionally wanted to have confirmed in *The Five Obstructions*. To that extent, von Trier did see what he 'wanted' to see. But, again, this is precisely why it is the view of others who stand in substantive relation to us that matter for the purposes of self-understanding. It is because they know us, have extended experience of our reactions and habits, that second-persons are so useful in this enterprise. It is no surprise at all that our intimates can formulate any number of predictions, about how we will be likely to behave in a given set of circumstances, that will indeed be confirmed in those circumstances.

Still, the letter is also correct in stating that von Trier is revealed in the film. For the expectations he has of Leth and his reactions to Leth's remakes point to facts about himself that he might otherwise not be able to access. The letter itself, written as it was by von Trier, can also be read as a kind of confession or admission. But whatever insights von Trier achieves, they would not have been possible without the collaboration of Jørgen Leth, unwitting though that particular collaboration might have been.

Lars von Trier: incurable romantic?

Watching *The Five Obstructions* reminds us of the familiar debate between romanticism and rationalism. As Leth contemplates remaking his film in Mumbai, he remarks:

> Lars von Trier has this romantic notion that I'll be so affected by being placed in a situation where social drama is going on beside you. He wants to quantify how much it rubs off, how much it affects me. Will it be visible? Will it be quantifiable? But I think it's pure romanticism. Obviously, there is no physiological law. There is no physical law that states that you can witness so much that you can reach the limit where you break down.

In subsequent interviews Leth has stated the following:

> Lars has this crazy theory that truth comes out if you are broken. And I don't agree with that. It is a romantic and sentimental notion. He wanted

me to break down. But it will not happen. Not with me. (Quoted in Brooks 2003)

I think [von Trier] has a purity complex. I don't believe in these ideas. I contest them. With this intelligence he is able to do such evil games. But I think it's a romantic notion that I don't agree with. But I think he's honestly very interested in the process of destructing ... in a religious way ... to rebuild everything. (Quoted in Kaufman 2004)

Von Trier, it is said, thinks that art comes out of messiness, from accidents. The thrust of Dogma 95 was spontaneity and honesty and real, direct emotionality. Cool, cerebral Leth would appear to be the opposite of this. But, ironically, *The Five Obstructions* serves to undermine von Trier's romanticism. There are no wholly self-made selves. Any human self, perhaps especially a creative human self, is not and cannot be a solipsistic construction. Crucially, we need others to understand ourselves. Neither Jørgen Leth nor Lars von Trier can escape this simple fact.

NOTES

1   I do not mean to suggest that documentaries are, by their nature, genuinely objective representations. Like any other human creations they bear, to a greater or lesser degree, the imprint of their creators' interests. Nor do I mean to have exhausted the moral questions that arise with respect to documentary filmmaking. For more on these issues see, for example, Gross *et al.* 1988.

2   This, by the way, is why my focus is on the role of *second*-person perspectives rather than on any old third-person perspectives. Individuals stand in only the most trivial relations to third persons. In particular, a third person, C, can have a perspective on first person, A, without being in any substantive relation with A, for example being in dialogue or participating in a joint activity.

3   Very roughly, the idea is that autonomy comprises a set of capacities which an individual can possess to greater or lesser degrees and which they are able to exercise with greater or lesser confidence. Like our other capacities, autonomy and agency develop over time in particular individuals in particular social and physical

environments. Some of the latter will be conducive to flourishing in this area and others not.

4 Leth recreates the dinner scene (of all things!) in the middle of the road. The people of the area are visible behind a semi-transparent screen erected behind Leth sitting at the table.

WORKS CITED

Brooks, Xan (2003) 'The Pupil's Revenge', *Guardian Unlimited*, 7 November. Available at: http://browse.guardian.co.uk/search?IDim=3D4294962719%2B3097&search=xan+brooks&No=10&year=2003&search_target=%2Fsearch&N=4294962719&fr=cb-guardian (accessed 2 October 2006).

Corliss, Richard (2004) 'Five Different Pieces', *Time*, 163, 7 June, 23.

Gross, Larry, John Stuart Katz and Jay Ruby (eds) (1988) *Image Ethics*. New York and Oxford: Oxford University Press.

Kaufman, Anthony (2004) 'Breaking von Trier: Jørgen Leth Survives *The Five Obstructions*', 26 May. Available at: http://www.indiewire.com/people/people_040526.html (accessed 2 October 2006).

Levine, Andrew (2004) *The Day My God Died*. Available at: http://www.pbs.org/independentlens/daymygoddied/film.html (accessed 16 October 2006).

Mark, Mary Ellen (1981) *Falkland Road: Prostitutes of Bombay*. New York: Alfred Knopf.

Menen, Rajendar (2001) 'The Ironies of Kamathipura', *The Hindu*, 3 June. Available at: http://www.hinduonnet.com/thehindu/2001/06/03/stories/1303128f.htm (accessed 16 October 2006).

Merleau-Ponty, Maurice (1962) *Phenomenology of Perception*, trans. Colin Smith. London: Routledge and Kegan Paul.

Meyers, Diana T. (1989) *Self, Society, and Personal Choice*. New York: Columbia University Press.

Nedelsky, Jennifer (1989) 'Reconceiving Autonomy: Sources, Thoughts, and Possibilities', *Yale Journal of Law and Feminism*, 1, 1 (Spring), 7–16.

Ricoeur, Paul (1966) *Freedom and Nature: The Voluntary and the Involuntary*, trans. Erazim Kohak. Evanston: Northwestern University Press.

Scott, A.O. (2004) 'A Cinematic Dual of Wits for Two Danish Directors', *The New York Times*, 26 May, E5.

Style and Creativity in *The Five Obstructions*

METTE HJORT

'Style' is one of those terms to which we regularly have recourse, with self-confidence and ease, in everyday conversation. Persons are often said to have a certain style, understood as a characteristic way of behaving that can be identified as pleasing, off-putting, charming or engaging, as the case may be. We regularly describe buildings, or people's ways of inhabiting them, in stylistic terms, just as we are confident that we know what we mean when we speak of people making certain lifestyle choices. However, if we shift our attention from the language of everyday interaction to that of a specialised and disciplined analysis or appreciation of the arts, the apparently self-evident meaning of 'style' quickly gives way to competing discourses and rival definitions. There is considerable disagreement about what the concept of style actually entails, and at times serious doubt has even been cast on the value of having such a concept in the first place. David Bordwell remarks, for example, that the stylistic analysis of film has been associated with untenable doctrines of aesthetic autonomy and the formalist research programmes to which such doctrines gave rise (1997: 5). The aim here cannot be to provide a satisfactory general account of style that settles the many thorny issues that are part of this concept's effective history. The far more modest goal is to shed light on a particular aspect of the phenomenon of cinematic style: the relation between creativity and style.

An influential view, associated with Richard Wollheim, has it that 'every *artist* [as compared with a mere practitioner of a given art] has an individual style' (Ross 2003: 236). Individual style is thus typically aligned with inventiveness and innovation, with creativity in some sense of the term. Yet little has been said about how we are to understand creativity. Nor has there been much discussion of the fact that style, under certain circumstances, can become an obstacle to creativity. In an argument aimed at establishing the undesirability of attributing several different styles to any given artist, Wollheim does recognise the possibility of various problems arising in connection with the expression of style. When faced with work that does not obviously correspond to a given style-description, we are urged to take the following possibilities seriously: 'the artist has not as yet formed his style, or the work is prestylistic; the artist has suffered a loss of style, or the work is poststylistic; the artist draws upon different parts of his style in some of his works, or the relevant work is style-deficient' (1979: 144). What might be involved in losing a style or in creating works that are style-deficient is not, however, spelt out. In some instances, I suggest, such problems occur as a result of a given film practitioner's excessive commitment to individual style understood primarily as the production of discernible or salient regularities. To understand what goes wrong in such cases we need to pay special attention to the *temporality* of individual style, but we also need to understand that style is not ultimately reducible to salient regularities.

The Five Obstructions, a philosophically-minded experiment involving Danish filmmakers Lars von Trier and Jørgen Leth, contributes a number of key insights to the discussion of film and style. Analysis of this work shows, more specifically, that (i) salient regularities can be the mark of creativity at one moment in time and an obstacle to creativity at a later moment in time; (ii) style, narrowly understood as discernible regularities, can be the cause of a loss of style in a broader sense; and (iii) a loss of style that arises in this manner is a problem that can be resolved through strategies involving the obstruction of preferred practices and the imposition of new rules for creative production.

To focus on individual style as an expression of, but also potential problem for, creativity is, it strikes me, a useful thing to do, particularly if it can be a matter of exploring a concrete model for creative practice that offers some possible solutions. Evaluative talk about the efforts of film directors often turns on the positive and negative aspects of individual style. Younger directors such as Thomas Vinterberg or Vincent Chui are castigated for failing in subsequent works to meet the stylistic expectations that *The Celebration* (*Festen*, 1998) and *Leaving in Sorrow* (2001) respectively created. If works such as *It's All About Love* (2003), *Dear Wendy* (2005) or *Fear of Intimacy* (2004) disappoint it is partly because they fail to deliver further stylistic signs of genuine creativity. Wong Kar-wai, on the other hand, disappointed many critics and fans when the long-awaited *2046* (2004) turned out to be a pastiche-like work that recalled several of his earlier films. The acquisition of a distinctive style, and the practice of style as a properly creative rather than merely repetitive process, are tasks that film practitioners working with some concept of film as art necessarily confront. And in some filmmaking contexts, especially those associated with small nations, the failure to succeed at these tasks registers as more than a purely individual problem. As an issue with genuine practical reality and wide-ranging consequences, individual style and its relation, or lack thereof, to creativity deserves a place within the ongoing discussion of cinematic style.

I would like to begin by piecing together a workable definition of individual style before turning to *The Five Obstructions*. Definitions of creativity, as we shall see, are much more straightforward and can be easily provided at the appropriate moment in the discussion of this important film.

Individual style and cinematic authorship

I have been qualifying 'style' with the term 'individual' and it is time to say a few words about the implicit contrast with other types of style, as well as about the implications of individual style for conceptions of cinematic authorship. As Bordwell remarks, style, understood as a 'systematic and significant use of techniques of the medium' (1997: 4) takes many forms. The term 'style', he points out, may be used with reference to a single film, with reference to the work of a particular individual, or in connection with the films of a group or collective. Discussions of the style of Hou Hsiao-hsien or Kim Ke-duk would, according to this view, count as explorations of individual style, whereas analyses of the Dogma 95 movement or the somewhat related Sixth Generation phenomenon in the People's Republic of China would involve group style. According to Wollheim, who is often cited in connection with the distinction between individual and general style, the group style that Bordwell identifies would be one of three types of general style – school style, period style and universal style – all of which are to be contrasted with individual style (1995: 40). Analogies for the pictorial examples that Wollheim provides might include the style of Zhang Yimou (as an instance of individual style), the style of the Fifth Generation Chinese filmmakers (as an example of school style), the style of spectacular Chinese heritage filmmaking (as an instance of period style) and, finally, heritage filmmaking (as an example of universal style).

The decision to focus on individual style, rather than on some version of general style, requires some justification, and not only on account of influential arguments to the effect that films reflect dominant social structures and pervasive ideologies rather than the workings of individual agency. The fear, more specifically, might be that discussions of individual style necessarily commit us to untenable views on cinematic authorship as ultimately a form of single authorship. Berys Gaut (1997) has identified some of the problems that a defence of cinematic authorship as single authorship entails. The restriction strategy that Gaut associates with Robin Wood, Richard Wollen and Victor Perkins aims to construe the contributions made by collaborators as artistically irrelevant, and thus to reserve authorship for the director and the artistically relevant contributions that he or she makes to the filmmaking process. The sufficient control strategy associated with Perkins involves first conceding the collaborative point about most filmmaking in order then to assert that a director qualifies as a film's author by virtue of being 'chiefly responsible for the effect and quality of the completed movie' (quoted in Gaut 1997: 157). The construction strategy associated with George Wilson and others similarly accepts the collaborative nature of filmmaking. In this case the author returns as a postulate that must necessarily be made if cinematic texts are to be properly understood and appreciated. There is not enough time here to reconstruct the details of Gaut's various objections to these three strategies. Suffice it to say that his rejoinders hinge on showing (i) that any audio-visual element encountered in a film is potentially artistically relevant and significant (1997: 156); (ii) that control in film is a complicated matter inasmuch as 'the dimensions of variation' that are possible when performing the tasks of filmmaking 'are immense' (1997: 157); and (iii) that postulated authors would have to be creatures of such 'protean talent' (1997: 160) as to be altogether too remote from everyday conceptions of human agency as to be convincing. Gaut does concede that creative power may be more or less centralised in a given instance of filmmaking, and that some filmmaking processes may be more consensual than others, the implication being that intuitions having to do with hierarchies of command and executive control will be relevant in some cases. This is an important point and probably one that needs to be more explicitly incorporated into Gaut's conception of cinematic authorship as multiple.

In the present context, however, the aim is not to settle questions concerning the nature of cinematic authorship, but to show that a concept of individual style in no way rests on broadly auteurist premises. Gaut concludes his discussion by suggesting that films, rather than being rigidly categorised 'by their directors', 'should be multiply classified: by actors, cameramen, editors, composers, and so on' (1997: 165). The idea, clearly, is that films can be discussed in terms of the contributions of multiple agents, all of whom have an individual style if, we might add, they are gifted at the tasks for which they are responsible. Far from being at odds with a view of cinematic authorship as collaborative, individual style is a means of demonstrating the validity of the multiple authorship thesis.

Individual style, salience and discernability

But what, more specifically, is style? Individual cinematic style, we may assume, is manifested in cinematic works. But what form does this manifesting take and are there less immediately apparent factors to which we should also be attentive as we seek to identify a given film practitioner's individual style? Bordwell's definition of film style allows us to begin to respond to these questions: 'I take style to be a film's systematic and significant use of techniques of the medium. Those techniques fall into broad domains: *mise en scène* ...; framing, focus, control of colour values, and other aspects of cinematography; editing; and sound. Style is, minimally, the texture of the film's images and sounds, the result of choices made by the filmmaker(s) in particular historical circumstances' (1997: 4). Bordwell rightly points out that style may also involve 'other properties, such as narrative strategies or favoured subjects or themes' (ibid.). In this regard his account of style accords with Nelson Goodman's influential discussion in 'The Status of Style', where the claim is made that 'What is said, how it is said, what is expressed, and how it is expressed are all intimately interrelated and involved in style' (1978: 29).

Shifting attention from the patterns of continuity and change that figure centrally in Bordwell's historical discussion of style, we might be tempted to assume that individual style amounts to discernible properties manifested with such regularity in a given oeuvre as to be characteristic of the relevant film practitioner's uses of the medium. Yet there is an influential view that holds that it is a mistake to equate individual style with discernible regularities. As Wollheim famously puts it: 'some stylistic features may be such that they can be detected in a given work only with great difficulty. Stylistic features need not be obviously present when they are present, and the possibility should always be entertained that there will be some stylistic features that, so far from acting as clues to authorship, can be detected only once authorship has already and independently been established' (1979: 143). Individual style, in short, is not the same thing as a readily legible 'signature'. The point of insisting on a distinction between individual style and signature is not to trivialise characteristic regularities as important elements of individual style, but to ensure that properly contextual factors bearing on the various psychological realities that are generative of individual style receive due attention.

An example might be helpful at this point. As an accomplished, innovative and prolific director, Lars von Trier is the kind of film practitioner who can be expected to have developed an individual style. While *Element of Crime* (1984), *Epidemic* (1987), *Europa* (1991), *Breaking the Waves* (1996), *The Idiots* (*Idioterne*, 1998), *Dancer in the Dark* (2000), *Dogville* (2003) and *Manderlay* (2005) may be individually characterised by significant uses of the techniques of the cinematic medium, these uses are by no means obviously systematic across works. With the exception of *Dogville* and *Manderlay*, analyses of style at the level of the individual films do not produce the kind of redundancies that might justify the attribution of a particular individual style to the director. That this should be so is no accident. Von Trier puts the point as follows: 'You can become so good at producing things that they become nauseatingly boring to look at. That might have happened had I continued to make the same film again and again, as some people do' (quoted in Hjort & Bondebjerg 2001: 213). The commitment throughout, it transpires, is to a form of self-provocation that involves *abandoning* the cinematic techniques as they are mastered in favour of new challenges. What persists across the corpus is an underlying involvement with filmmaking as a series of rule-governed experiments designed to test certain hypotheses: the idea that creativity depends on obstructive constraints in *The Idiots*; the idea that intensely sentimental stories can become the vehicle for artistic contributions in *Breaking the Waves*; the idea that the musical can be made the vehicle for powerful emotions in *Dancer in the Dark*. An adequate Lars von Trier style description would have to take into account the kind of constitutive rules that govern the director's various experiments, yet these are by no means immediately discernible in the way that the use of voice-over narration, hand-held cameras or multiple immobile cameras might be in a given film. Style, then, combines discernible with less obviously discernible properties, and this, as we shall see, is a premise that underwrites the solution to the problem of style as an obstacle to creativity in *The Five Obstructions*.

Style as act

A filmmaker's style, then, may not always take the form of recurrent audio-visual properties, but may instead manifest itself in the more general cinematic acts that provide a constitutive framework for a given film. There may be a consistency of vision that is articulated most clearly through 'framing acts' that have a shared core even as they generate quite different craft-related challenges requiring diverging solutions and thus diverse rather than convergent visual effects. An act-based approach to cinematic style can contribute something useful to the understanding of individual cinematic style, but primarily through the study, where relevant, of acts that have an overarching, second-order or framing dimension. To date the so-called adverbial or act-centered approach to style has neglected such framing gestures in favour of highly particularist analyses of the way in which techniques are used, and of the types of actions to which such uses amount (see Ross 2003: 237). Thus, for example, a proponent of the view that style inheres in artistic acts might have us note that Hitchcock uses highly dissonant extra-diegetic music in the opening scenes of *Vertigo* (1958) to *characterise* the fall of the policeman as *traumatic* for the James Stewart character, Scottie. The music 'modifies' the scene, to use Noël Carroll's (1996) term, as traumatic. It is not clear to me that the act-centered approach, when practiced in this manner, really delivers on the idea that style inheres in acts rather than the manifest properties of works. Oftentimes, it seems, the proponent of the adverbial approach ends up simply describing manifest properties in a way that accords with pragmatic theories of language and communication. What *is* useful, in my view, is an extension of the act-centered approach to constitutive frameworks, as a way of explaining the less obviously discernible elements of style.

Style, intention and knowledge

If significant film practitioners can be assumed to have individual styles, then to what extent are these styles a matter of conscious intent or lucid self-understandings? In *The Transfiguration of the Commonplace*, Arthur Danto argues that style is a gift and cannot be learned, unlike manner which can be acquired. Whether something qualifies as style rather than manner, claims Danto, depends on whether it originates in art or knowledge, art being associated with style, knowledge with manner. Style, following Danto, is quite simply an expression of an individual's 'ways of seeing the world' (1981: 204). Inspired by Schopenhauer, Danto claims that 'the style of a man is … the physiognomy of the soul' and goes on to suggest that 'if style is the man, greatness of style is greatness of person' (1981: 205, 207). In addition to downplaying the role of learning, Danto builds an important element of opacity into his person-centred definition of style. He puts the point as follows: 'the outward aspects of representations are not commonly given to the man whose representations they are: he views the world through them, but not them' (1981: 207).

The insistence on opacity is also evident in Wollheim's work on style. He situates his discussion of individual style within a psychological and intentionalist framework, intention being equated 'with more or less any psychological factor that motivates' a given artist to engage with his art in 'one way rather than another' (1995: 39). Style is held to involve two types of capacities or skills, 'schemata' and 'rules or principles for operating with these schemata' (1995: 42). In the context of cinema the schemata might include precisely those elements to which Bordwell refers – framing, focus, *mise-en-scène*, editing – while the principles might include ideas about continuity editing, analytic editing or Soviet montage. The artist's schemata, as well as the rules that tend to govern their mobilisation, are believed by Wollheim to be a matter of tacit knowledge. This commitment to tacit knowledge has clear implications for the role of conscious intention in the development and manifestation of individual style. Following Wollheim the artist need not have 'direct access to the processes of style … Indeed, there is no reason to think that [the artist] has any mental representation of his individual style, either in an overall way or in its detail or structure' (1995: 48).

A somewhat more catholic perspective than that advocated by Danto and Wollheim seems advisable when it comes to understanding the psychological dimensions of individual style. In some instances properties that are deemed to be significant indicators of style are consciously available to the artist in the form of describable techniques, solutions and driving concerns, all of which come together in some kind of self-reflexive narrative about individual style. In other cases such indicators may well be the result of inarticulate processes that have not been made the object of an introspective act of mental representation. My suspicion is that most significant film practitioners have a partial, rather than full, understanding of the ways in which their practices generate a form of individual style, and that very few operate with tacit knowledge only. Films make their way into the world, where they are discussed and analysed, often in stylistic terms. The conversations that unfold in the course of a work's reception may enhance an artist's reflexive awareness of salient elements of individual style, which may in turn have ramifications for his or her subsequent output. Individual style is, then, best thought of as combining conscious and tacit dimensions, with the tacit elements tending towards explicitation as a result of the dynamics of reception. *The Five Obstructions*, we shall see, suggests that certain creative problems produced by style can be resolved through a therapeutic process aimed at bringing some of the tacit or unconscious dimensions of individual style to conscious awareness.

Let me turn, then, to the film itself.

The Five Obstructions

The Five Obstructions shows the two filmmakers meeting at Zentropa in April 2001. They watch Leth's starkly minimalist, black and white, experimental short film from 1967, which von Trier claims to have seen around twenty times. Having watched *The Perfect Human* with Leth, von Trier states the ostensible purpose of the remake exercise: 'That's a little gem that we are now going to ruin', which Leth claims to consider a 'good perversion' that is worth 'cultivating' (Mark Jenkins' review for the *Washington Post* indicates that the film is 'unrated' and 'contains a few brief sexually explicit scenes and much film-theory perversity' (2004)). *The Five Obstructions* documents the exchanges between von Trier and Leth in which the former articulates the obstructive rules, Leth's attempts in various parts of the world to work with the rules, and von Trier's responses to the remakes that Leth produces. The viewer sees the results of Leth's efforts and enough of the original short film to be able to engage in evaluations of the works' relative merits.

What, we might ask, is the point of engaging in an obstructive game that is ostensibly aimed at somehow ruining an artistically successful film? Von Trier, I have argued elsewhere, is fascinated by the concept of gifts, by good gifts and bad gifts, and by the ways in which the dynamics of a gift culture more generally can generate the kind of surplus value that is particularly important in small-nation contexts (see Hjort 2006). *The Five Obstructions*, it turns out, is in the final analysis a kind of gift from von Trier to Leth, or this, at least, is what the impresario von Trier would have us believe. In the concluding moments of the film, von Trier makes the following statement on the grounds of the Film Town in Avedøre, where the Zentropa offices are located: 'There are just a few areas in life on which I think I'm an expert. One of them is Jørgen Leth. I think I know considerably more about him than he does.' The entire exercise, von Trier smilingly remarks, was essentially a 'Help Jørgen Leth project', a gift flowing from von Trier to Leth.

Concepts of game behaviour, gifts, sacrifice and therapy dominate the two filmmakers' meta-discursive comments, some of which are made within the context of the work that *The Five Obstructions* amounts to, others in discussion with film critics and the press. Leth, for example, provided the following characterisation of the game that he took himself to be embarking upon with von Trier: 'So we are entering a game – but not a sweet children's game. It will be full of traps and vicious turns' (Danish Film Institute 2002: 32). In many ways the game in question is a psycho-therapeutic one, with all of the attendant power plays, some of them quite poignant since it is a matter of the younger pupil, von Trier, adopting the role of therapist in relation to his former teacher, Leth. As part of his response to one of Leth's remakes, von Trier explains his intentions as follows: 'It's similar to therapy … Why go, if you don't give the therapist the cards? My plan is to proceed from the perfect to the human. That's my agenda. I wish to "banalise" you. By finding things that hurt. The soft spots.' Leth, von Trier repeatedly insists, is stubbornly refusing to create something that is less than perfect, something that would be at odds with his preferred self-understandings as a filmmaker and artist. Yet it is precisely some form of imperfection that von Trier seeks as a kind of 'gift' or 'sacrifice' from Leth. Leth remains unscathed and 'unmarked' by the obstructions, says his opponent, yet what the game requires is a willingness to be exposed, to be vulnerable, to fail: 'The greatest gift an actor can give you' as a director, von Trier insists, 'is to fuck up. I want the same kind of gift as I get from an actor when he does a scene in a way that he hates.'

Let us take the recurring references to gifts seriously and ask how *The Five Obstructions* might be seen as helping Leth. There is the sociological point to be made that von Trier's collaborative initiative effectively leverages Leth into a sphere of international visibility by means of the gift of reputation. Leth's comments in interviews focusing on the success of *The Five Obstructions* reveal that he is very much aware of this aspect of the project. More interesting in the present context, however, are the gifts of talent and friendship that von Trier makes Leth and, more importantly still, the gift of creativity. Responding to Leth's first remake, *#1: Cuba*, von Trier remarks that the most diabolical of the imposed obstructive rules was a 'gift' and that the result was like watching 'an old Leth movie'. Talking to Leth in Haiti from Copenhagen following a synchronised viewing of Leth's *#4: Cartoon*, von Trier indicates that he himself will produce the final film. We will look at the rules governing this particular remake in the conclusion to this discussion. What is relevant at this point is von Trier's final remark in the phone conversation: 'You won't have to do anything, so don't worry, you can go ahead and lose yourself in your Haitian depression' (Leth lives in Haiti and has done so since the early 1990s).

Leth published his memoirs, *The Imperfect Human*, in autumn 2005, and in this book – a *succès de scandale* that has had dire consequences for its author – there are long discussions of Leth's struggle with depression, and of the ways in which a network of friends, including the painter Per Kirkeby and his then wife, the former Zentropa film producer Vibeke Windeløv, tried to help him. Leth describes at some length how he was rescued from a kind of depressive paralysis by the then director of the Danish Film School, Henning Camre, who simply ordained that he would start teaching the new intake of students at the Film School within 48 hours. This intake included figures who have since become central in the New Danish Cinema – Thomas Vinterberg, Per Fly and Ole Christian Madsen – and it was through them, claims Leth, that he rediscovered an interest in life, and a creative impulse fuelled by the reciprocities of the teaching process (see Leth 2005). Camre, incidentally, is a long-time friend of Leth's, having served, for example, as cinematographer for Leth's experimental documentary entitled *Life in Denmark* (*Livet i Danmark*, 1971).

My point is this. There is every reason to believe that Lars von Trier, who himself struggles with depression and who has known and admired Leth for many years, genuinely thought of *The Five Obstructions* as a form of artistic therapy. The project has a number of features that are noteworthy in this connection. The collaborative dimension, which brings the pleasures but also the responsibilities of friendship into play, resolves the kind of commitment problem that depressive paralysis generates in relation to individual initiatives. The conception of the project as involving a series of remakes, rather than just one, introduces an extended temporal horizon that allows the effects of the therapeutic game genuinely to take hold. And, finally, the obstructive rules are themselves designed by an insightful friend and talented filmmaker who has thought long and hard, not only about differences between early and more recent Leth films, but about the conditions that make creativity possible. The key rules imposed by von Trier, we shall see, serve the purpose of obstructing elements of style that have become, with time, mere manner, equivalent to a loss of style.

Let us look more closely at the relation between the obstructive rules that von Trier imposes and some of the style descriptions that Leth reflexively provides in an interview conducted by Mette Hjort in 1998 (see Hjort & Bondebjerg 2001). Leth's descriptions, as we shall see, encompass the full range of stylistic possibilities, referring both to his philosophy of filmmaking and to its practical implications for his way of using the resources of the cinematic medium. Von Trier's Obstruction #1 reads as follows: '12 frames, answers, Cuba, no set.' Put less succinctly, the first rule specifies that any shot included in the film can be no more than 12 frames; the second rule requires Leth to answer the voice-over questions that accompany the images in the original film; location shooting on Cuba is imposed in a third rule when Leth admits to never having been to the island; and a set is finally ruled out when Leth enthusiastically expresses his intention to rely on a set in his first remake.

While location shooting in Cuba and without a set emerge as a result of the dynamics of the two filmmakers' interaction, the first two rules are more obviously connected to Leth's track record as a filmmaker. Leth, we learn, is unperturbed by the second, third and fourth rules, but seriously unsettled by the first. Documentary images show Leth fuming against the 12-frame rule, which, he believes, is designed to 'ruin' the film 'from the start'. Von Trier, Leth insists, has set things up in such a way that he, Leth, will have to make a 'spastic' film.

Arguably the result of careful thinking on von Trier's part, the first of the four rules reveals the logic that drives von Trier's game. The aim, more precisely, is systematically to target some of the discernible regulari-ties that are likely to figure centrally in any style description associated with Leth. A particular use of the long take is, as Leth himself points out, a recurrent feature of his filmmaking practice, an expression of his philosophy of time, and a reflection of the creative influence that other artists have had on him: '[John] Cage's philosophy of emptiness, the way he utilises temporal duration, have left definite traces in my films. It's a matter of having confidence in simplicity, in every single minute, in time as it passes. Cage's ideas are reflected in the confidence I invest in the long take, where the contemplation of time and events within a single frame goes on for quite a while' (quoted in Hjort & Bondebjerg 2001: 61–2). Referring to the scene in *66 Scenes from America* (*66 scener fra Amerika*, 1981) in which Andy Warhol eats a hamburger and then says, 'Ah ... My name is Andy Warhol and I just finished eating a hamburger', Leth points out that 'the scene has three gifts':

> First of all, there is the temporal duration itself, which makes it a pure Cage scene. Time passes and things happen, and the action in question is very simple and at the same time very expressive and full of plasticity. Then some light falls through the window, a sunray changes the image twice by altering the light on Warhol's face. This is a pure gift ... Finally, Warhol happens to misunderstand what he's supposed to do, so there's a long pause after he's finished eating his hamburger during which time he simply sits there, ready ... At last after a noticeable pause, he says the phrase and the explanation for the delay is that he was waiting for a cue. Now, this delay gives the scene a quite different dimension ... At some level, I really believe in a kind of magic of the film material. (Quoted in Hjort & Bondebjerg 2001: 70–1)

Leth's understanding of time as stochastic and potentially creative recalls Cornelius Castoriadis's (1987) views on socially significant time or kairotic time as a dynamic source of newness. Given the connection between Leth's long-take practice and his understanding of the sometimes magical and nonintentional dynamics of creativity in filmmaking, it is not difficult to see why von Trier's 12-frame rule registers as the imposition of a truly alien framework.

Leth's cinematic oeuvre includes fiction films and documentary works, and his reputation in Denmark and elsewhere as an innovative experimental filmmaker rests primarily on films such as *Life in Denmark*, *66 Scenes from America*, *Stars and Watercarriers* (*Stjernerne og vandbærerne*, 1973) and *A Sunday in Hell* (*En forårsdag i helvede*, 1976), all of which are contributions to the documentary genre. Von Trier's second obstruction targets Leth's characteristic attitude as an experimental documentary filmmaker, and some of the cinematic practices through which it finds expression. The exchange about this set of obstructive rules develops as follows:

Von Trier: The highly affected distance you maintain to the things you describe, that's what I want to get rid of in my next obstruction ... I'd like to put your ethics to the test ... We talk so much about the ethics of the observer.

Leth: The observer is my role, of course. It's my instinct.

Von Trier: I want to move you on from there. To make you empathise. ... Would you film a dying child in a refugee camp and add the words from *The Perfect Human*?

Leth: No, I'm not perverse.

Von Trier: But there is a degree of perversion...

Leth: ...in the distancing.

Von Trier: How far are you willing to go if you're not describing something? Would anything rub off?

The rules are finally formulated as follows: 'The most miserable place; don't show it; Jørgen Leth is the man. The meal.' Leth, that is, is to remake his film in a truly miserable place and is to find some way of doing this without making the misery part of the film's pro-filmic material.

Leth is himself to play the role that the actor Claus Nissen played in the original film. The remake will focus on the sequence in which Nissen wears a tuxedo and eats a gourmet meal, the implication being that Leth must consume such a meal in the midst of misery that cannot be directly shown. The point is to see whether the surrounding poverty, illness and exploitation of the Bombay red light district, where Leth opts to shoot his remake, will appear indirectly in the images in the form of discomfort, embarrassment, empathic involvement or a deeper crisis of conscience.

In Obstruction #2 all four rules combine to challenge the disengaged, distanced or analytic quality of Leth's documentary style. Leth is very aware of this aspect of his visual style and provides a detailed description of it in the same interview quoted above. Once again, we note, Leth sees an intimate link between the discernible regularities of his works, in the form of a systematic use of the techniques of the cinematic medium, and a more general artistic self-understanding. If Cage helps to explain Leth's use of the long take, the films of Jean-Luc Godard and the writings and photographs of Bronislaw Malinowski shed light on Leth's way of composing images and his use of captions or voice-over narration. Referring to Godard, Leth identifies the influence of what he calls 'a pseudo-anthropological approach to reality': 'I've ... written about Godard's films ... describing his pseudo-anthropological approach to reality, which is also my own. It's a question here of adopting a stance towards reality that is marked by wonder, questioning and to some extent naïveté, while at the same time adopting a stance towards film that makes possible a probing, analytic and experimental relation to the language of film and its capacity to describe reality' (quoted in Hjort & Bondebjerg 2001: 61). What is appreciated in the case of Malinowski is the ethnographer's distanced style: 'I see anthropology and especially Malinowski as tools that I can use in my films ... What fascinates me about Malinowski is actually his use of language and the distance – the very precise distance – he establishes in relation to his subject matter' (quoted in Hjort & Bondebjerg 2001: 62). Leth is not alone in noting that Malinowski's preference for 'horizontally-framed [frontal] shots taken from a middle distance' (Young 1998: 17), and for series allowing for the exploration of a single subject from multiple viewpoints, creates a distanced and generally analytic effect.

Leth's disengaged third-person observer stance finds expression in a desire to dissect everything 'in an almost experimental manner' (quoted in Hjort & Bondebjerg 2001: 63). It underwrites a related inclination to ask 'the most awkward questions' (ibid.), even if, we surmise, such questions transgress the boundaries of propriety or challenge the ethical limits that common sense places on art's treatment of the real. The distanced, analytic gaze, we note, may at times be self-reflexive, as it is in *Notes on Love* (*Notater om kærligheden*, 1989), which includes scenes with Leth as well as some framings of Malinowski's photographs from the Trobriand Islands. Referring to his role in front of the camera in this film, Leth makes the following point: 'I'm fascinated with this idea of performing an action while at the same time observing myself doing it. There's a kind of "schizophrenia", if you will – which is perhaps part of life too – in both my poetry and my films' (quoted in Hjort & Bondebjerg 2001: 65). At times the sense of distance is the result not only of the way in which the image is composed, but of the relation between word and image. Relevant in this regard is the significantly delayed voice-over in *66 Scenes from America* or the categorical titles in *Life in Denmark*, a film that recalls Malinowksi's composition of the image as well as his approach to word/image relations: 'My references [to Malinowski] go all the way back to *Life in Denmark*. That is, when I line up the women in that film, I'm drawing on Malinowski. Indeed, there's actually a hidden reference to Malinowski: it's almost a citation. The subtitle reads 'Women from a Provincial Town', and both the composition and title recall Malinowski' (quoted in Hjort & Bondebjerg 2001: 63). Referring to *66 Scenes from America*, Leth notes his fascination with 'the idea of pushing the way in which the image is read in different directions', and with the thought that 'the very gesture of providing information can have the effect of categorising an image' (quoted in Hjort & Bondebjerg 2001: 70). Cage, Warhol and Marcel Duchamp inform Leth's thinking about the former idea, but it is Malinowski's visual style that suggests the latter.

I have discussed the first two sets of obstructive rules at some length, and will describe Obstructions #3 and #4 more succinctly, so that I can move on to my theoretical points about creativity. Leth returns from Bombay with a film that is rejected by von Trier on the grounds that it does in

Leth's Malinowski-inspired approach to image and text in *Life in Denmark* – 'A provincial town'

'Young unmarried women…

…from a provincial town' (*Life in Denmark*)

fact show the 'miserable place', albeit through a translucent screen. Leth is instructed to return to the city, which he refuses to do, and von Trier thus imposes punishment in the form of a free-style film instead. Given that von Trier has claimed, time and again, to have learnt the importance of constraints or rule-governed frameworks for filmmaking from his former teacher, Leth, the free-style film Obstruction #3 imposes can only be a straightforward negation of Leth's characteristic approach. Obstruction #4 requires Leth to remake *The Perfect Human* as an animated film. As a citizen of a welfare state with generous subsidies for filmmakers, Leth is well aware that he has had the luxury throughout his career of remaining true to the artistically uncompromising idea of making only films that genuinely excite him as a film practitioner with experimental inclinations. Obstruction #4, von Trier knows, imposes a filmmaking task that is bound to provoke revulsion and thus to transform the motivational basis for Leth's filmmaking in this particular instance. In Obstruction #4 von Trier explicitly targets the pleasure that Leth normally takes in filmmaking, and the opening moments of the fourth remake show a slow moving tortoise accompanied by Leth's voice-over utterance of the word 'ulyst', 'disinclination'. There is a fifth obstruction, as the title suggests and as mentioned above, but I shall save this one for my concluding remarks, as it serves a somewhat different function within the overall project.

Let me try now to draw the theoretical lessons on individual style and creativity that are embedded in *The Five Obstructions* experiment. In this regard it is important to note that Leth's four remakes are truly remarkable and genuinely inventive. That the experiment is effective is more than evidenced by the works with which Leth returns, and Jonathan Romney (2003), writing for the *Independent on Sunday*, does not hesitate to assign victory to Leth in an article tellingly entitled 'Lars von Trier, nil. Jorgen [sic] Leth, five'. If the point of *The Five Obstructions* was to stimulate creativity then there can be no doubt about the experiment's success. But what exactly are the cogent theoretical principles that allow it to succeed? The first principle is that constraints provide the conditions for creativity. This is an idea that has been explored at some length by Jon Elster (1992, 2000), who proposes to view constraints as imposed, invented or chosen. The second principle is that the overarching framing acts and attitudes that constitute the less obviously discernible aspects of individual style can inform a wide range of practices that register as discernible properties of cinematic works. The third principle focuses on the causes of style loss: if a virtually automatic link between general attitudes and specific discernible properties arises and becomes almost second nature for the film practitioner, a once properly creative individual style becomes mere manner and a derivative, reflexive imitation of individual style. The result is a loss of style. The fourth principle is that creativity can be rediscovered and style recovered through the mobilisation of rules that are at once invented and imposed. The filmmaker who has suffered the loss of style is a passive agent – a mere patient – in this regard, for it is a question of merely consenting to imposed constraints with no possibility for input. Yet the constraints that are imposed are at the same time invented, in a spirit of solidarity and friendship, by a knowledgeable colleague with a clear sense of where attitude and practice have become so tightly connected as to undermine the creativity of individual style. While the invented constraints are merely imposed from the point of view of the passive patient, these constraints are *informed* by what the active agent takes to be the deeper interests of the individual whose loss of style is to be remedied. A further intuition seems to be operative in the experiment, namely, the thought that the formulation of properly therapeutic invented constraints requires a collaborator, the creative disorder being precisely beyond the lucid purview of the patient.

If we turn to the philosophical literature on creativity, we soon discover that the assumptions about creativity and style that are operative in *The Five Obstructions* find considerable support in writings by leading experts on the subject. A few select references to Margaret A. Boden's (1994, 2004) work suffice to illustrate this point. Boden distinguishes between what she calls historical and psychological creativity. 'Historical creativity' is a term that she reserves for acts that have never, in the course of history, been performed before, whereas 'psychological creativity' is used to refer to acts that may well replicate earlier acts, but which are novel when viewed in relation to the relevant agent's earlier actions. Radical psychological novelty arises when a given individual's 'conceptual space', understood in terms of constitutive rules unifying and structuring a domain of action and thinking, is somehow transformed. Creativity, in short, hinges on the transgression or rejection of at least one of the constitutive rules. In most instances, the task of transforming a given conceptual space falls squarely on the shoulders of the individual who aspires to be genuinely creative and to be recognised as such. Settling on the particular way in which the principles are to be thwarted or abandoned is typically assumed to be integral to, rather than a mere precondition for, the genuinely creative act. The premise underwriting *The Five Obstructions*, however, is that it can be helpful in cases of style loss to shift the burden of transforming conceptual space to the shoulders of an insightful collaborator. Von Trier's rules quite simply impose a transformation of Leth's conceptual space, and in so doing they create the conditions that will automatically incline Leth to abandon a style-cum-manner in favour of new ways of expressing the experimental stance that is ultimately the basis for his distinctive style.

I would like to conclude with a few brief remarks about the fifth obstruction, which reads as follows: 'Lars von Trier will make the last obstruction. Jørgen Leth will be credited as director. Jørgen Leth will read a text written by Lars von Trier.' The text in question takes the form of a letter in which the Leth persona constructed by von Trier claims victory over von Trier, whose ruses have been all too transparent throughout. It is von Trier, rather than Leth, the voice-over claims, who has been obstructed and exposed in all of his abject humanity. If *The Five Obstructions* is genuinely a 'Help Jørgen Leth' project, then why, we might ask, does von Trier orchestrate a remake that assigns unambiguous victory to Leth over von Trier? The answer, I think, is quite clear. There are, as we know, certain kinds of gifts that can only be accepted if there is some kind of opacity involved, the case of anonymous giving being an obvious example. The gift of creativity, in the form of an externally reconfigured conceptual space, will only have lasting effects if the recipient understands it in terms other than univocal, unidirectional giving. The last obstruction scrambles the rules governing the experiment and subverts the metaphor of therapy with all of its attendant notions of dependency and hierarchy. It is useful here to recall Blaise Pascal's analysis of the phenomenon of conversion in his *Pensées* from 1670. It is possible, Pascal claims, to trick oneself into becoming a true believer. If, however, the faith that results from the strategic manipulation of personal beliefs is to count as lasting faith, then the element of strategy must at some point in the process disappear from mental view. Belief is not true belief as long as its manipulative origin remains accessible to the conscious mind. The last obstruction serves to introduce a similar element of opacity that is critical in this instance to the success of the therapeutic project. If the problem of style loss is to be lastingly remedied through a gift that prepares the ground for psychological creativity, then the manner-breaking creativity of the therapeutic remakes cannot be viewed by Leth as *primarily* externally generated. By assigning unilateral victory to Jørgen Leth, the last obstruction obscures the deeper purpose of the obstructive rules and makes available a narrative of victory and success. The retrieval of individual style, Lars von Trier seemingly understands, depends as much on confidence and a powerful sense of self-efficacy as it does on the reconfiguration of conceptual space.

WORKS CITED

Boden, Margaret A. (ed.) (1994) *Dimensions of Creativity*. Cambridge, MA: MIT Press.

_____ (2004) *The Creative Mind: Myths and Mechanisms*. London: Routledge.

Bordwell, David (1997) *On the History of Film Style*. Cambridge, MA: Harvard University Press.

Carroll, Noël (1996) *Theorizing the Moving Image*. Cambridge: Cambridge University Press.

Castoriadis, Cornelius (1987) *The Imaginary Institution of Society*, trans. Kathleen Blaney McLaughlin. Cambridge: Polity Press.

Danish Film Institute (2002) *Film: Special Issue / Leth*. Copenhagen: Danish Film Institute.

Danto, Arthur (1981) *The Transfiguration of the Commonplace*. Cambridge, MA: Harvard University Press.

Elster, Jon (1992) 'Conventions, Creativity, Originality', in Mette Hjort (ed.) *Rules and Conventions: Literature, Philosophy, Social Theory*. Baltimore: Johns Hopkins University Press, 32–44.

_____ (2000) *Ulysses Unbound: Studies in Rationality, Precommitment, and Constraints*. Cambridge: Cambridge University Press.

Gaut, Berys (1997) 'Film Authorship and Collaboration', in Murray Smith and Richard Allen (eds) *Film Theory and Philosophy*. Oxford: Oxford University Press, 149–72.

Goodman, Nelson (1978) 'The Status of Style', in *Ways of Worldmaking*. Hassocks: Harvester Press.

Hjort, Mette (2006) 'Gifts, Games, and Cheek: Counter-Globalisation in a Privileged Small-Nation Context: The Case of *The Five Obstructions*', in Claire Thomsen (ed.) *Northern Constellations: New Readings in Nordic Cinema*. Norwich: Norvik Press, 41–59.

Hjort, Mette and Ib Bondebjerg (2001) *The Danish Directors: Dialogues on a Contemporary National Cinema*. Bristol: Intellect Press.

Jenkins, Mark (2004) 'Five Obstructions: Filmmaker Faceoff', *Washington Post*, 26 March. Available at: www.washingtonpost.com/wp-dyn/articles/A24183-2004Mar25.html (accessed 10 January 2005).

Leth, Jørgen (2005) 'Ubeslutsomhed', extract from *Det uperfekte menneske. Scener fra mit liv, Weekendavisen*, 23–29 September,1, 12.

Pascal, Blaise (1954 [1670]) *Pensées*, in *Oeuvres Complètes*. Paris: Gallimard, 1081–345.

Romney, Jonathan (2003) 'Lars von Trier, nil. Jorgen [sic] Leth, five; *The Five Obstructions*', *Independent on Sunday*, 9 November. Available at: http://find-articles.com/p/articles/mi_qn4159/is_20031109/ai_n12749633 (accessed 10 January 2005).

Ross, Stephanie (2003) 'Style in Art', in Jerrold Levinson (ed.) *The Oxford Handbook of Aesthetics*. Oxford: Oxford University Press, 228–44.

Wollheim, Richard (1979) 'Pictorial Style: Two Views', in Berel Lang (ed.) *The Concept of Style*. Philadelphia: University of Pennsylvania Press, 129–45.

_____ (1995) 'Style in Painting', in Caroline van Eck, James Mcallister and Renee van de Vall (eds) *The Question of Style in Philosophy and the Arts*. Cambridge: Cambridge University Press, 37–49.

Young, Michael W. (1998) *Malinowski's Kiriwina: Fieldwork Photography 1915–1918*. Chicago: University of Chicago Press.

Constraint, Cruelty and Conversation

HECTOR RODRIGUEZ

The motivation for writing this essay developed out of three overlapping concerns. The first was related to the emerging field of game studies. I had just completed an essay about the relationship between play and seriousness (Rodriguez 2006); this topic is the subject of an ongoing debate. Some scholars claim that playing is essentially not a serious activity, but a voluntary interruption of everyday affairs; it is fundamentally a diversion from the more pressing business of living one's life. Those who defend this thesis regard games as artificial formal systems purposefully isolated from the world. Others claim that playing can be a vehicle of education, social change, self-transformation and other serious aims. Games are, from this point of view, intimately intertwined with deep questions of life. My essay analyses in some detail Johan Huizinga's seminal book *Homo Ludens* (1998), which is often understood as an extended argument on behalf of the thesis that play constitutes a realm apart, a 'magic circle' strictly segregated from quotidian goals and interests. I conclude that Huizinga calls attention to the boundary between the playful and the serious only to show the fluctuating and ambiguous status of this distinction. The playful is not always and everywhere cleanly demarcated from the serious.

The second area of concern that underpins the present essay pertains to the role of constraints in the creative process. A constraint is a limitation or obstacle voluntarily accepted by the artist. The writers of the Oulipo group, such as Raymond Queneau, Italo Calvino, Georges Perec or Harry Matthews, advocate working within self-chosen constraints. Perec, for instance, set for himself the task of writing a novel, *A Void*, without ever using the letter 'e'. What is important is the obvious difficulty of this mission. Writing a book without the letter 'x', for instance, would not have posed much of a challenge because of the relative infrequency of the letter in English-language use.[1] For the writers of the Oulipo collective, creative work largely presupposes the establishment of an obstacle or challenge as a productive impetus to creative activity. They saw their work as essentially ludic, since every game forces the player to struggle against some artificial obstacle, so this idea ties up with my ongoing interest in the study of play. The Oulipo group is central to my own work as a practicing digital artist. Recently, I have been closely involved with the Writing Machine collective founded by Linda Lai; this group, one of the most promising initiatives in the current Hong Kong media art scene, has also promoted the value of self-chosen constraints as a major artistic approach.[2] The work of this collective raises the following question: whether generative or constraint-based artworks must always comprise tightly closed formal systems, or whether (and how) formal constraints can also open up the work to the life that is lived while making it.

The third set of concerns that inspired this essay arose in response to the film *The Five Obstructions*. I view this work principally as the occasion for a rich interpersonal interaction, at once playful and profoundly serious, between the two filmmakers. *The Five Obstructions* is an unfolding conversation. Its artistic content and value is inseparable from the dialogic process of its production; its subject matter is the kind of life that is being lived in the act of making it. More specifically, the film documents a sequence of challenges. Director Lars von Trier asked his long-time friend and mentor Jørgen Leth to remake Leth's influential 1967 short film *The Perfect Human* no less than five times, each under a different set of stringent conditions. Thus von Trier requires his mentor to shoot his film in Cuba and India, to keep the length of every shot down to 12 frames, to make a cartoon version, and to fulfil other increasingly more demanding constraints. Each 'obstruction' was designed as a trial for Leth. It is the nature of a challenge that it might not turn out as expected. *The Five Obstructions* is the opposite of a carefully pre-designed or storyboarded film, the style, structure and themes of which have been fixed in advance by its auteur; instead, it was deliberately set up as a creative and open-ended adventure. The viewer invariably experiences the film as a process whose outcome was not premeditated. This openness corresponds to an important concern of von Trier's, which perhaps manifests itself most strongly in *The Idiots* (*Idioterne*, 1998): his belief that cinema should extend the authors' (and also the viewers') ways of thinking and perceiving, leading beyond ordinary frames of expectation towards the new, the unseen, the unthought. Instead of treating cinematic style as a closed formal system, the aim is to open the cinema to the outside, to the flesh-and-blood richness of human life. This attitude of extreme receptivity and openness to the outside defines the only model of filmmaking that I find worth pursuing and celebrating. I feel a mounting dissatisfaction with the questions of visual style, narrative form and thematic meaning, which constitute the core content of a traditional cinema studies curriculum. Films are often treated as closed systems of form or meaning. There is nothing inherently false or unethical about this way of thinking, but its hegemony has sealed off other ways of reflecting about the act of cinema. I prefer instead to view the cinematic both as a ludic activity, closely connected to the study of games, and as a process of working through very serious matters pertaining to the care of the self and its relation to other people.

The starting point for this essay is the concept of play, which runs through the three concerns that motivated the writing of it.

The excellent study *Man, Play, and Games*, written by the French sociologist Roger Caillois (1961), contains an extended treatment of the relationship between playing and constraint. Its fundamental assumption is that there are two ways of playing, which Caillois famously calls *paidia* and *ludus*.

Paidia is characterised by a free and spontaneous enjoyment. It has an impromptu, uncontrolled and disorderly quality that is linked to sensory stimulation. Many living creatures relish the immediate experience of changing sounds, colours, movements and other physical sensations. Obvious examples include a dog sniffing a bone, a cat entangled in a blanket, a child making bubbles and a toddler responding with laughter at the sound of a rattle. The active exploration of, and interaction with, objects becomes a source of joy. Children grasp, drop, throw, smell and taste all sorts of things. There is a love of sheer surprise, motion and change. Moreover, this type of activity is essentially improvisational. Caillois is not primarily thinking of jazz musicians or actors whose improvisations rest on a solid foundation of sophisticated techniques and conventions. Pure *paidia* is impulsive and effortless. Skills, discipline, challenge and training are not involved. This form of free enjoyment is for Caillois the original form of playful activity.

The second mode of playing, *ludus*, grows *out of paidia*, when children deliberately set arbitrary challenges for themselves, such as, for instance, throwing a ball into a basket. *Ludus* denotes any system of rules deliberately designed to generate a *gratuitous obstacle or challenge* for the player. The difficulty is the point of playing. The obstacle is gratuitous in the sense that it has been set up solely for the pleasure of overcoming it. According to most theorists, games (as opposed to other forms of playing) largely consist of rule systems designed to establish arbitrary challenges, which the player voluntarily sets out to conquer. In his book *The Grasshopper*, for instance, Bernard Suits describes the action of playing a game as 'the voluntary attempt to overcome unnecessary obstacles' (1978: 41). A golf player cannot, for instance, simply grab the ball, walk to the hole and drop it in; instead, he must patiently keep on striking the ball with a club. It would be profoundly misleading to claim that the objective of golf is to introduce the ball into the hole. The point of playing the game is to overcome the difficulties brought about by the rules of the game, and so to overcome a challenge that has been conventionally established. The achievement of the final goal is pointless independently of the framework of rules that calls for skill, patience and effort. Suits describes the player's voluntary submission to an arbitrary rule system as the adoption of a 'lusory attitude' (1978: 35). The lusory attitude consists in choosing to accept the rules of the game, just so that the activity afforded by such rules can be carried out.[3]

The game player goes through a challenge that puts her intelligence, resistance, inventiveness, strategy, courage and endurance to the test. *Ludus* contains a strong element of suspense. When that tension is absent, the purpose of the action has been defeated. Consider the multiplayer game *MazeWar*, which requires players to shoot each other while moving about inside a maze. Some players discovered that they could easily make themselves invulnerable simply by positioning themselves inside a dead end and, facing the only entryway, shooting every passerby. This strategy, which is not technically in breach of the rules of the game, exploits a loophole in the rules to circumvent the challenge. Game designer Chris Crawford has observed: 'This behaviour was perfectly legal within the framework of rules, but everybody knew it was "not fair"' (2003: 39). Crawford's point is that the ultimate goal is not 'to beat the system enclosing the challenge' by achieving the objective in conformity with the formal rules; the objective is to conquer the challenge itself. The player must pass the test, not circumvent it. Those who exploit loopholes in the system are thereby betraying the spirit of the game, even if they are not technically violating the letter of its rules. The element of difficulty is essential, and so a game cannot be described as only a formal system, independently of the abilities and limitations of human players.

Ludus consists of sharply differentiated conventions, tools and resources that require specialised skills. Specialisation is crucial. This ludic spirit already underpins the first 'games' that children are capable of naming, such as, for instance, hopscotch, rope jumping, cops and robbers, hide-and-seek, tic-tac-toe, and so forth. The rise of *ludus* also manifests itself in other activities, which are not always described as games but which nonetheless present a distinctly specialised character, such as kite-flying or skateboarding; each activity displays distinctive conventions and utensils distinguishing it from other forms of play. Each must be learnt, and each presents some difficulty for the player. The rise of *ludus* out of *paidia* consists in the differentiation of children's play into distinct games; this process brings about an essential transformation in the nature of play, which becomes conventionalised and, in a (nonpejorative) sense, institutionalised. *Ludus* constitutes an enrichment of play, which acquires progressively more refined and diversified resources and concerns. Caillois' deep point is this: the acquisition of new resources – such as materials, utensils, technologies, goals and strategies – changes the internal quality of play. These resources are not external decorations; they are constitutive of the intrinsic experience of a ludic action. Crucially, they must be learnt. Wherever there is *ludus*, there is the possibility of training, the acquisition and refinement of skills. Whereas pure *paidia* cherishes effortless gratification, *ludus* requires effort, patience and practice. The player may gradually master the operation of a tool, such as a kite or a yo-yo, or more abstract reasoning skills like the ability to solve puzzles or mysteries.

Additional examples of games with strong *ludus* elements include crossword puzzles, mathematical recreations, anagrams, mazes, rope jumping, pinball machines, sports and most role-playing games. Hobbies like the meticulous construction of scale models or the invention of new gadgets also require persistence and self-discipline. Hacking can also be viewed as a form of *ludus*, since it is often done purely for the sake of mastering a difficulty. The player of *Grand Theft Auto: Liberty City Stories* who undertakes several taxi missions to improve his/her driving skills is thereby enjoying the element of *ludus* that is obviously central to the game. Some digital games, for example *Omikron: The Nomad Soul*, include shooting galleries where players can take time fine-tuning their skills. Many computer adventure games begin with relatively simple missions, such as driving a car to a particular location or throwing simple objects, all designed to train the player in such basic game mechanics as character motion and weapon handling. Playing a game requires patience, concentration, training and discipline.

To highlight the importance of *ludus* is to emphasise the importance of constraints in all forms of adult playfulness. In particular, the concept of constraint remains an essential feature of many forms of artistic production. Artists often work within a system of norms, such as the rules of poetic rhyme and pictorial perspective, the division of literature and film into narrative genres with fairly strict rules, or the codification of specialised musical forms like the sonata or the canon. Artistic equipment, such as a musical instrument or a photographer's camera, can also be considered as the physical embodiment of a set of constraints that must be mastered. These constraints are all received by the artist in the form of codified traditions that are recorded, taught and learnt.

Although the evolution of constraints clearly enhances human culture, the joyful improvisation characteristic of *paidia* nonetheless remains a vital aspect of adult play and creativity. It persists as a source of unruly spontaneity even in the midst of highly disciplined games. The contrast of *ludus* and *paidia*, then, is not an exclusive opposition. Even computer games like the *Grand Theft Auto* series, which require extensive skills in driving or shooting, also allow players the immediate pleasure of exploring a sprawling urban environment by, for instance, undertaking small missions or simply walking and driving around. This exploratory craving for perceptual discovery retains a strong element of *paidia*.

There is another sense in which *ludus* is sometimes intimately connected with *paidia*. The copresence of both aspects is essential to the nature of certain cultural activities whose main characteristic is this: improvisation and spontaneity are prominent, but only when the agent has mastered the requisite skill to the degree that its performance becomes automatic. In the case of improvisational music and acting, for instance, the person undertakes creative actions which are at once spontaneously performed and skills-based. Excellence in Chinese calligraphy calls for training, and yet its performance is often executed rapidly, before the ink dries up. Perhaps the combination of improvisation and spontaneity is a core aspect of all forms of play. Consider the case of skateboarding. On one hand, its performance clearly demands special skills acquired and refined through persistent exercising. On the other, the activity also involves a high level of moment-by-moment improvisation; the urban skateboarder must cultivate a state of alert readiness to respond to the unexpected. Moreover, this effort is motivated by a desire for intense and immediate physical sensations arising from gliding, leaping, and so forth, and thus manifests the fascination with perceptual change and surprise that Caillois identifies as essential to *paidia*. This intertwinement of skill and spontaneity also figures prominently in documentary filmmaking. The filmmakers must understand fully the operation of the camera and sound recording equipment; yet they must respond immediately to the ongoing contingencies of unpredictable situations, and embrace the value of surprise and novelty. Improvisation is central to most documentaries. (Theoretical discussions of documentary cinema, which tend to focus on epistemological questions about truth, objectivity and authority, often ignore the role of improvisation in the filmmaking process.)

Spontaneity is not incompatible with constraint. The very possibility of spontaneous action may in some cases require the presence of strong constraints. Spontaneity is something that, sometimes, we must work towards. This can be illustrated with reference to the so-called 'fundamental rule' of Freudian free association. Freud would ask his patients to report whatever would spring to mind, even when it might appear irrelevant, embarrassing or offensive. The free flow of ideas is thus guaranteed by a constraint. The purpose of the constraint is in this case to provide a framework for the spontaneous access to unconscious ways of thinking. Improvisation is here not only compatible with but also made possible by the existence of a constraint. It is even possible to conceive of a constraint stating that there should be no constraints. In *The Five Obstructions*, for instance, von Trier once lays down the rule that there should be no rules.

Ludus and *paidia* are also intertwined in another set of cases, those in which the constraints themselves evolve spontaneously, through some sort of improvisational action. To explain what is involved in this type of ludic action, I need to introduce the concept of a self-generated constraint.

Although constraints are primarily mediated through traditions, some artists prefer to devise their own systems of norms. The invention of such self-generated constraints has played a prominent role in contemporary art. Abstract painter Piet Mondrian deliberately restricted his colour scheme to black, white and the subtractive primaries (blue, yellow and red); he also eschewed all curves and diagonals and used only sharply delimited geometric forms. In his mature films, Japanese filmmaker Yasujiro Ozu avoided fades and dissolves, working largely with straight cuts, little or no camera movement and mostly low viewing positions. These two artists deliberately restricted the range of choices available to them.

It would seem that self-generated boundaries set strict limits on the spontaneity of the agent, but self-generated constraints sometimes evolve spontaneously. Consider the following instance: in a classical game situation, every player knows every rule in advance of the start of play. The rules have been fixed beforehand and all participants voluntarily submit to them. But it is possible to conceive of a game whose rules do not precede – but rather arise during – the playing of the game. Players might start out with only a few basic constraints and evolve the rest of the rules through a free-flowing conversation. The point is not how players here respond to the rules, but how they create the rules in the first place. Those norms might conceivably remain provisional and subject to revision throughout the process of playing. In this situation, players would have to negotiate the rules of their interaction. As I have noted elsewhere: 'The experimental emergence, sustenance and transformation of community would thus become the core subject and aim of the game' (Rodriguez 2006). I would now add that another possible topic of such a game is the display of the self, insofar as it unfolds in relation to the needs and judgements of others. The game may be designed so as to put friendship, love, trust, confession, suspicion, betrayal and other aspects of *intimacy* and *self-disclosure* into play. To elaborate on this aspect of serious play, I propose to consider the concept of self-generated constraint at greater length.

In particular, I want to examine some of the reasons why artists might choose to invent their own constraints. The decision to work within a system of self-chosen limitations has been justified by philosophers and artists in terms of five principal motives.

Some abstract painters sometimes assert that artistic beauty radically differs from natural beauty. Mondrian's self-imposed restrictions were designed to avoid any colours, lines and shapes that might possibly recall those in the natural world. Whereas nature dazzles the eye with varied forms and shades of colour, Mondrian restricted his vocabulary to a rigid set of basic elements. The use of exact and closed contour lines and the restriction of the artist's colour palette resulted in perceptual experiences radically different from those available in a natural setting. In general, the creation of artificial constraints can thus be used to highlight the conventional nature of artistic systems.

A second viewpoint justifies the construction of constraints as an assertion of freedom. The philosopher Jon Elster has expressed this rationale eloquently: 'If we regard an action very generally as the outcome of a choice within constraints, then typically the choice will represent an element of freedom and the constraints an element of necessity. If, however, the constraints themselves are freely chosen, the element of necessity is to some extent mastered and harnessed to a purpose'[4] (1984: 80). In a superb monograph, David Bordwell has drawn on Elster's discussion to describe the films of Yasujiro Ozu as a deliberate narrowing down of the basic set of stylistic options available to him (1988: 162–3). He views Ozu as a filmmaker who purposefully restricted his choices by setting up intrinsic norms and developing ludic variations on these norms. Insofar as it is self-imposed, this restriction is not a loss of freedom but rather an assertion of it.

The voluntary limitation of resources can also be viewed as a way for the artist to focus her attention in a manner that could be loosely described as experimental. The designer of an experiment typically maintains certain features rigidly constant in order to observe the effect of varying a limited set of parameters. The existence of carefully designed constraints is thus a core aspect of experimental action. Its purpose is to eliminate the effects of irrelevant factors and to maintain a situation of control. Modern artists have sometimes adopted an experimental research agenda. Painter and educator Josef Albers spent years primarily painting squares, in order to concentrate his activity on the perceptual effects of different relations between colours.

The construction of a new constraint can be seen as a vehicle of artistic progress, as the invention of a new technique. Each new constraint is a novel artistic resource made available to the artistic community. This can be seen in the work of the members of the Oulipo group, who saw themselves as inventors of new techniques that augment the repertoire of literary techniques.

The Oulipo writers also celebrated constraints as antidotes against romantic values like inspiration and self-expression. In their view, an important aspect of creative work is the artist's voluntary submission to a system of limitations. I have always found this idea extremely fruitful in my teaching: whenever students find themselves thwarted by a creative block, waiting helplessly for some mysterious source of inspiration, it is useful to suggest that they should let some arbitrary constraint guide the execution of the work. Why not try, for instance, to make a comic book that can be read upside down, diagonally, or following the movement of a knight in chess? The confrontation with an artificial difficulty is an important source of artistic ideas. This idea is relevant to *The Five Obstructions*, which can be described as the process whereby one filmmaker (von Trier) helps another (Leth) to overcome an artistic block, precisely by setting up a series of constraints.

Artists and philosophers have, then, described and justified the invention of new constraints with reference to at least five goals: (i) distinguishing art from nature; (ii) affirming the artist's freedom or mastery; (iii) concentrating the artist's attention on an experimental research agenda; (iv) enriching art by discovering new techniques; and (v) undermining the importance of inspiration in art-making. In addition to these five aims, *The Five Obstructions* brings out another way of thinking about the role of constraints. To understand what is involved here requires that we reconsider the question of difficulty in creative activity. In what ways can artistic activity be difficult?

Most discussions assume that a difficult task is demanding on our intellectual or physical skills. Its execution requires training and effort. Making a perspective drawing, for instance, is time-consuming; dancing and skateboarding call for long hours of arduous practice. But some activities are difficult because we deeply resist doing them. Scholars who analyse games often forget that people do not always find playing pleasurable: children sometimes experience sports as deeply intimidating; some adults treat games involving close physical contact with other players as either repugnant or embarrassing. There is such a thing as *resistance* to playing. Another activity that many people fear entering into is psychoanalysis, which requires from the patient an attitude of submission to strict constraints, such as the discipline of keeping appointed times, attending sessions regularly and (especially) speaking freely about one's experiences. Psychoanalysis is difficult *because we are not inclined to conform to those constraints*. The source of the fear is not the constraints themselves but the experiences with which the constraints are designed to bring us face to face. The frightening nature of these experiences is revealed in the insistent efforts patients frequently make to bargain their way out of the rigours of therapeutic dialogue.

The concept of resistance has not, to my mind, been sufficiently discussed in the literature on aesthetics. An activity can be difficult not only because it requires a high level of manual or intellectual skill, but also because it is deeply feared. The nature of the difficulty lies in our resistance to the activity. Working through this resistance essentially calls for an interpersonal situation. What is resisted – the source of the patient's fear in a therapeutic situation – is the experience of being exposed intimately to another person. This is very different from the sort of difficulty involved in solving a mathematical puzzle or composing a musical canon. It is the sort of difficulty involved in *The Five Obstructions*. One feature of this type of interpersonal situation is that compassionate concern cannot always be definitely disentangled from cruelty and the thirst for power. To describe what is involved in more concrete terms, it is illuminating to consider the film in some detail.

The Five Obstructions documents a conversation between friends. The nature of this conversation, the unpredictable ebb and flow of its ongoing dynamic, is the subject of the film. Both filmmakers start out by agreeing on a basic, overarching constraint: Leth agrees to fulfil the tasks stipulated by von Trier, however unreasonable they might appear to be. The content of each task is not, however, agreed upon at the outset. Von Trier often invents new rules on the spot, in response to casual comments made by Leth. When Leth mentions his love of Havana cigars, for instance, his friend immediately stipulates that the next film must be shot in Cuba. One filmmaker spontaneously makes a constraint out of the remarks spontaneously proffered by the other. Some constraints are based on von Trier's long-term knowledge of his friend; for instance, his requirement that one film should consist only of 12-frame shots reflects his awareness that Leth prefers a long-take style. Throughout the film, von Trier adopts a special attitude towards the utterances of his friend, regarding them as raw materials with which to elaborate a new constraint, and Leth becomes increasingly more cautious as he realises that anything he says may be turned against him. The interplay between self-revelation and the formation of constraints is perhaps the core mechanism of *The Five Obstructions*. Too much critical attention has been devoted to the ways Leth responds to the obstructions stipulated by von Trier; few commentators have ad-

Lars von Trier spars...

dressed the process whereby those constraints were conceived in the first place. The five obstructions emerge out of a conversation. The constraints are thus spontaneously generated, bringing together *ludus* and *paidia*.

The Five Obstructions provides a model for creativity as ludic action. Its basic feature is the spontaneous generation of constraints in a situation of intimate conversation. But the dialogue is essentially conflict-ridden. An 'obstruction' is not exactly the same as a 'constraint'. The term suggests something like the clash of two footballers on opposite teams, one person deliberately blocking the advances of another. Thus the interplay of force and counter-force is crucial here. If there is a ludic element, it is profoundly agonistic; it recalls games of competition. The five obstructions are stages in an active confrontation. Von Trier clearly enjoys taunting and provoking his friend. He sees himself as the originator of the idea and the driving force behind its execution, assertively placing himself in the position of a teacher and a psychoanalyst, and he clearly relishes the position of authority that he has reserved for himself. The ethos of this project is obviously very far removed from the love of intellectual games and mathematical puzzles characteristic of the Oulipo group.

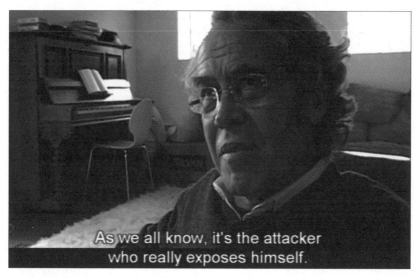

As we all know, it's the attacker who really exposes himself.

...with Jørgen Leth

A crucial aspect of the dialogue is the element of subjection. From the very start, Leth agrees to conform to the constraints put into place by von Trier, who likes to speak of 'self-flagellation' and 'sacrifice'. He describes his obstructions as having a twofold aim. The first is to hurt his friend. But hurting him is not enough. The tasks are also designed, secondly, to make a deep mark in Leth's character. One of the obstructions, which obliges Leth to visit a red light district in Bombay, is meant to question the director's detached, observational style – which von Trier regards as a carefully engineered and cultivated pose – by confronting him with a situation of extreme misery. In *The Five Obstructions*, the principal task for Leth is not to make a series of good films but to fulfil obediently the requirements set for him. Subjection, not the pursuit of aesthetic value, is the core focus of the enterprise. Leth often attempts to circumvent the task at hand by interpreting it loosely, bargaining his way around it or evading it altogether. But for each task there can be success or failure, and the absolutely final test is von Trier's acceptance or rejection of whatever film Leth brings back. The master's instructions cannot be interpreted loosely: 'It was not the film I asked for,' is his devastating reply to one of

Leth's projects. The film that his friend had ended up making, von Trier acknowledges, is probably superior to the film actually requested, but the aesthetic quality of the product is not the point. Von Trier is particularly concerned to prevent his friend from hiding behind a façade of cleverness, feigned indifference or sensuous beauty.

In this context, questions of ethics naturally come to the foreground, because of the obvious possibility that one person might take advantage of the other. Von Trier's obstructions often have an element of sadistic aggression. The line between hostility and compassionate care is difficult to define with any degree of certainty. Von Trier explicitly states that the project's basic conception was a personal attack against his friend and mentor, and yet it was also meant kindly. Throughout *The Five Obstructions*, the boundary between aggressivity and kindness is often blurred. This ambivalence gives the peculiar character of cruelty to the film.

Elaborating on this element of cruelty, von Trier adds that he only chastised his friend because he himself desired chastisement, so his aggressiveness can be viewed as a form of projective identification. It was from the start an act of martyrdom, displaced onto another person. In some sense, one could read this element of projection as a metaphor for a certain form of cinematic masochism. In fiction films like *Breaking the Waves* (1996) or *Dancer in the Dark* (2000), von Trier portrays characters, often women, undergoing painful humiliations, and these characters can all be seen as projective fulfilments of the filmmaker's deep-rooted desire for self-flagellation. But the documentary format of *The Five Obstructions* introduces an important variation to this projective scheme. The other person is not a fictional character wholly created by the author-god but an autonomous person who can actively resist von Trier's attacks. In a newspaper interview, Leth himself criticised von Trier's conviction that truth only arises through extreme humiliation: 'Lars has this crazy theory that truth comes out if you are broken. And I don't agree with that. It is a romantic and sentimental notion. He wanted me to break down. But it will not happen. Not with me' (quoted in Brooks 2003). Leth clearly sees himself as resisting his friend's attacks. The autonomy of the other is an important ethical (and also artistic) aspect of the film. The viewer is always aware that *The Five Obstructions* lacks a single authorial voice. It is not the case that a filmmaker shapes a character in line with his own projective fantasies. The clash of subjectivities is a fundamental aspect of the work.

To recapitulate, *The Five Obstructions* gives a model of ludic interaction having the following features: the initial constraint, agreed upon prior to the start of the game, stipulates that one filmmaker (the 'subject') will implement the restrictions imposed by the other (the 'game master'). The latter will judge what does or does not count as a successful implementation. The actual gameplay consists of three core activities. The first is a series of conversations where the game master uses comments from the subject, as well as his own personal knowledge of the subject, to specify several tasks. The second activity consists of the efforts by the subject to fulfil those tasks. The third is the moment of judgement, whereby the game master decides whether or not the intentions have actually been fulfilled. Judgement is followed by a reward or a punishment. The game master has carefully designed this process deliberately to inflict pain, and also to make a permanent mark on the subject. The design must be based on the master's own personal familiarity with the subject, cemented through ongoing conversations. The master's psychological motivations are ambivalent, mixing cruelty and compassion. The subject chooses to resist this aggression by various means, such as evading or reinterpreting the task, refusing to speak words that might reveal his true feelings, and so forth.

Near the film's conclusion, von Trier mentions that perhaps he has seen only what he expected to see. This statement brings out a core theme of the film, the struggle within and against the cognitive schemata that frame our expectations. To view *The Five Obstructions* is to notice the ambiguities involved in one person's perceptions of the other. The entire project becomes a hall of mirrors, shot through with ambiguities,[5] which manifest themselves primarily in two areas. The first involves the power relation between the two filmmakers. The viewer becomes increasingly unsure about which person is actually directing the entire situation. Leth gradually appears to gain the upper hand; he grows progressively more self-confident, while von Trier's own self-assurance is progressively eroded. If *The Five Obstructions* is partly about the intertwinement of power and care, the nature of the power relation is difficult to describe precisely.

The second area of ambiguity pertains to the question of self-disclosure. Von Trier highlights this topic in the concluding segment of the film, which he himself directs but using Leth's name and Leth's voice-over: he describes the Leth persona as a carefully tailored fiction. Von Trier's stated aim was, at least in part, to penetrate the mask and undermine the fiction. But whose self is in the end really exposed? Whose personality is revealed? Perhaps the film exposes far more about von Trier's arrogance, and about his ambivalence regarding a key father figure in his life, than about Leth's own character. Von Trier notes: 'It is always the attacker who is exposed.' *The Five Obstructions* concludes on a note of failure: 'Nothing was revealed, and nothing helped.' The viewer emerges from this confrontation uncertain as to its outcome. Has the entire project really been a failure? What, if anything, has been learnt about the two artists? What, if anything, has changed in their lives? In this game of attack and counter-attack, power relations become ambiguous, and the success or failure of the entire project remains obscure.

Ambiguity is of course a familiar modernist trope. Some would say, no doubt with good reason, that it has become a pretentious and tiresome cliché. In *The Five Obstructions*, however, ambiguity does some very important work. As a first approximation, we might say that ambiguity calls attention to the fluidity of interpersonal situations. It is difficult to describe precisely who dominates whom, and it is difficult to separate the mask from the authentic self. This difficulty is not a matter of some contingent cognitive limitation on the part of either filmmaker; it is in the nature of an interpersonal situation that these determinations should remain essentially elusive. There are no precise or definite facts of the matter. The point of this indefiniteness is not, as another cliché would have it, to encourage viewers to 'think for themselves'. Rather, the point is to express an image of thought, a paradigm of what it means to think. More specifically, the film tackles the possibility of thinking thoughts that defy clear-cut categorisation. Thinking is not (at least not only) the application of a predefined image or schema that enables recognition and identification. Rather, thought is an opening to the new. Ambiguity is thus not an end in itself; it is an aspect of a mode of thinking as radical openness, without a predefined image. The philosopher Gilles Deleuze has expressed this point, which to my mind is the key to his entire oeuvre: 'the problem is not to direct or methodically apply a thought which pre-exists in principle and in nature, but to bring into being that which does not yet exist ... To think is to create' (1994: 147).

The making of *The Five Obstructions* is a work of thinking as problematising. As I have noted elsewhere, paraphrasing Huizinga:

> The etymological roots of the word 'problem' ... reveal two closely related meanings: 'problemata' were (a) shields used for protection and (b) things thrown for another person to grab hold of. The ideas of skill, competition and challenge are everywhere evident. The philosophical *aporia* or paradox, for instance, was originally understood as an enigma without a definite answer, often put forth as a challenge to a real or imaginary opponent. (Rodriguez 2006)

Each task is an open problem that von Trier aggressively throws at Leth. But the need for von Trier to invent each successive task also constitutes a problem, since the rules are not designed in advance. Thinking unfolds, as it should, in fits and starts, uncertain of its destiny, its path and its nature. Here we see the key point of the dialectic of *ludus* and *paidia*, of constraint and improvisation, in *The Five Obstructions*: it is about the origin of thinking as an open adventure, beyond mere recognition, out of a conflict-ridden encounter with a loved one.

NOTES

1 A comprehensive collection of Oulipoean techniques can be found in Motte Jr (1998).
2 See http://www.writingmachine-collective.net/blog/?page_id=11.
3 For an extended discussion of this topic, see Bradford (n.d.).
4 I am grateful to Paisley Livingston for a fruitful conversation about this topic.
5 He also notes that he is only putting words into his friend's mouth to avoid saying them himself.

WORKS CITED

Bordwell, David (1988) *Ozu and the Poetics of Cinema*. Princeton: Princeton University Press.

Bradford, Gwendolyn (n.d.) 'Kudos for Ludus Game Playing and Value Theory', *Noesis*, 6, 3. Available at: http://www.chass.utoronto.ca/pcu/noesis/issue_vi/noesis_vi_3.html (accessed 27 August 2007).

Brooks, Xan (2003) 'The pupil's revenge', *Guardian Unlimited*, 7 November. Available at: http://film.guardian.co.uk/interview/interviewpages/0,,1080386,00.html (accessed 27 August 2007).

Caillois, Roger (1961) *Man, Play, and Games*, trans. Meyer Barash. New York: Free Press.

Crawford, Chris (2003) *Chris Crawford on Game Design*. Indianapolis: New Riders.

Deleuze, Gilles (1994) *Difference and Repetition*, trans. Paul Patton. London: Athlone.

Elster, Jon (1984) *Sour Grapes: Studies in Rationality and Irrationality*. Cambridge: Cambridge University Press.

Huizinga, Johan (1998) *Homo Ludens: A Study of the Play-Element in Culture*. London: Routledge.

Mondrian, Piet (1951) *Plastic Art and Pure Plastic Art*. New York: Wittenborn.

Motte Jr, Warren F. (ed.) (1998) *Oulipo: A Primer of Potential Literature*. Normal, IL: Dalkey Archive Press.

Perec, Georges (1969) *La Disparition*. Paris: Éditions Denoel.

Rodriguez, Hector (2006) 'The Playful and the Serious: An Approximation to Huizinga's Homo Ludens', *Game Studies: The International Journal of Computer Game Research*, 6, 2. Available at: www.gamestudies.org (accessed 27 August 2007).

Suits, Bernard (1978) *The Grasshopper: Games, Life, and Utopia*. Toronto: University of Toronto Press.

Artistic Nesting in
The Five Obstructions

PAISLEY LIVINGSTON

Artistic nesting, or the display of one work of art by another work, has several important functions in *The Five Obstructions*, such as the obvious yet crucial one of advancing a story about filmmaking by acquainting the spectator with the relevant films. Nesting is what allows viewers of *The Five Obstructions* to respond directly to Jørgen Leth's cinematic accomplishments, and thereby reinforces one of the main points of the film, which is that Leth has successfully met Lars von Trier's challenge to make new versions of *The Perfect Human* under difficult and even objectionable circumstances. To express this point in terms introduced in the film, the nesting of *The Perfect Human* and the five new versions or 'obstructions' helps convey the idea that von Trier has failed to get the elder filmmaker to produce 'crap', just as he has failed to inflict upon him the supposedly 'therapeutic' experience of flailing about like a tortoise on its back. More importantly, the nesting of Leth's works makes *The Five Obstructions* succeed as a 'Help Jørgen Leth project', to evoke one of von Trier's more sympathetic statements of his goals.

In what follows I shall explore some of the ways in which nesting functions rhetorically and stylistically in *The Five Obstructions*. Firstly, I offer a general characterisation of the species of meta-representation known as nesting or embedding. Then I ask how nesting creates a context for both the making and reception of Leth's short films. Lastly, I set forth a paradoxical argument that arises with reference to authorship and collaboration in *The Five Obstructions*. A discussion of the conditions on individual and joint authorship makes it possible to avoid the paradoxical conclusion.

What is artistic nesting?

Briefly, a work of art nests another, actual or imaginary work of art just in case it displays at least part of its artistic structure (see Livingston 2003). This definition may seem simple enough, but some of its key terms and implications may require some elucidation. 'Artistic structure', for example, is Jerrold Levinson's term for 'all perceivable, appreciatively relevant components of a work' (1990: 162). The kind of relevance that Levinson has in mind here concerns the appreciation of a work of art as an *artistic* accomplishment (as opposed, say, to a financial or political one). And the structure of the work is only those parts of it that can be perceived with one or more of the five senses. Paint on the surface of a canvas that is put on public display is part of an artistic structure; most often, the back of that same canvas is not. In the case of the cinematic medium, the artistic structure is the artistically relevant parts of the pre-established or recorded sequence of moving images that in many cases are accompanied by a pre-determined sequence of sounds or music.

My definition of nesting requires that the matrix work *display* at least part of the artistic structure of a nested work. One way to couch this condition is to say that the artistic structure of the nested work, or at least part of that structure, must be depicted by or 'observable-in' the nesting or matrix work. This mode of depiction can be more or less transparent. When the artistic medium of the nesting work allows it, the nested work's structure, or part of that structure, is quite literally made perceptible in the nesting work, transparently and without loss. For example, when a novel accurately quotes the words of a poem, a faithful token of the poem's structure is directly and fully presented to the reader of the novel. Unless some special context has been established (for example, the

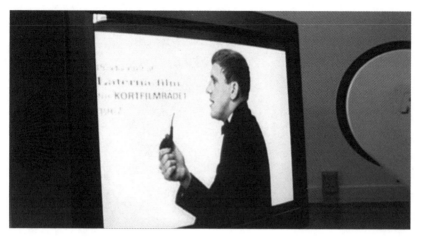

The video within the film

poem is a work of calligraphy), it would be inappropriate to complain that the nesting work had failed to give the reader a visual representation of the original manuscript of the poem. Similarly, due to its characteristic and remarkable representational or depictive capacities, the cinematic medium can quote or display the artistic structures of works in a wide range of media with perfect transparency. A film can, for example, give us a perfectly faithful experience of hearing some recorded music, looking at a photograph or seeing a work of calligraphy.

In some cases nesting is 'transparent', then, but in others the display is less direct as a result of differences in the media. The contrast I have in mind can be illustrated with reference to examples from *The Five Obstructions*. Early on in this film bits of *The Perfect Human* are shown by means of shots of a television monitor on which a video recording of *The Perfect Human* is being played. In these shots the television screen is shown from an angle; the monitor's image is blurry and the sound is unclear. Subsequently in *The Five Obstructions*, we are given direct, full-screen displays of segments from *The Perfect Human*, at which point the audio-visual display of *The Five Obstructions* is simply that of the relevant segment from *The Perfect Human*. The latter film is not, of course, quoted *in toto* in this manner in *The Five Obstructions*, nor are the bits that are shown presented in

Transparent nesting of shots from the dinner sequence

the same order in which they are presented in the original 1967 work. Yet with regard to any given segment re-presented in *The Five Obstructions*, the citation is perfect, as no artistically or aesthetically relevant features are left behind (as would be the case, say, in a moving picture image of a sculpture). As a result it would make no sense to say that *The Five Obstructions* only shows us 'copies' of *The Perfect Human*; what the spectator is given is in any case a projection or screening of a copy of *The Five Obstructions*. The same is true of the several new films that Leth and his collaborators are shown working on in the course of the film. These films are directly presented in *The Five Obstructions*, so that in seeing the latter work, one directly experiences these nested works.

Another distinction that may be drawn within the broad category of artistic nesting is relevant here. Artistic nesting can be either complete or partial in the sense that either the totality or only a part of a work's artistic structure can be made accessible to those who experience the matrix or nesting work. Spectators of *The Five Obstructions* see only parts of *The Perfect Human*; by contrast, they see all of each of the 'obstructions' (according to Leth; personal communication with Mette Hjort). Yet in the context of a viewing of *The Five Obstructions*, many spectators may have the impression that they are only seeing parts of much longer, nested works, just as the presentation of clips from the original film, *The Perfect Human*, is elliptical. In fact, the five obstructions are all roughly five minutes long (in contrast to the 13 minutes of the original), and when each of them is presented, the implication is that the spectators of *The Five Obstructions* have been allowed access to a film 'simultaneously' being experienced by Leth and von Trier.

The upshot of these points about the specific strategy of nesting adopted in *The Five Obstructions* is that it would apparently be absurd for a spectator to claim that he or she cannot assess Leth's achievement here because the new versions of *The Perfect Human* are unavailable. The immediate response to such a claim would be: on the contrary, the obstructions, or at least representative parts of them, are transparently put on display in the film. And this in turn supports my opening point about one of the main rhetorical functions of nesting in this film: the film co-directed by von Trier and Leth is designed to engage the spectator directly and immediately with Leth's achievement.

The situation, however, is not quite so simple. Even though the nesting is transparent, *The Five Obstructions* creates a very special context for the short films effectively displayed within it, and this context makes a difference to their appreciation – or so I shall argue in the next section.

Context and quality

To understand how the context and history of the making of a cinematic work makes a difference to its qualities, we must try to appreciate the same audio-visual sequences across two different contexts of production and reception. In other words, we take the same (types of) images and sounds and assess them in different contexts of creation, the one actual, the other possible. This is an approach made famous by Jorge Luis Borges (1939), and subsequently adopted by such prominent philosophers of art as Kendall L. Walton (1970), Richard Wollheim (1978) and Arthur Danto (1981).

Imagine, then, that Leth had independently taken the initiative to make four or so versions or remakes of *The Perfect Human*; imagine as well that these versions were precisely those that the spectator of *The Five Ob-*

structions is shown, namely, *#1: Cuba*; *#2: Bombay*, and so forth. The question, then, is whether in such a radically different context, works such as *#1: Cuba* would have had all and only the same artistic (stylistic, aesthetic) qualities as they have in the actual context, that is, the context where they are nested within *The Five Obstructions*. What I want to suggest is that in that alternative, 'counterfactual' context, each individual 'obstruction' would have a strikingly different status and set of artistic and aesthetic features from those it has in the actual context of *The Five Obstructions*. A hypothesis to be explored is that these versions have, on the whole, more valuable and interesting artistic features in the latter, actual context than they would have had in the former.

Let us label the conjunction of those two ideas the 'strong contextualist thesis' – namely, the claim that the context not only makes a difference to the qualities of the embedded works, but in this case makes them better. For the sake of convenience, I shall, in what follows, provide some labels for the distinct contexts I have in mind. Let 'Leth's avant-garde cinema' refer to a context in which the filmmaker independently takes the initiative of making and displaying films to be broadly situated within an avant-gardist cinematic tradition; such a context, which is that of the largest part of Leth's cinematic works, can be contrasted to the context established by the storyline of *The Five Obstructions*, namely, a context in which the new versions of *The Perfect Human* are to be viewed and evaluated as the products of a collaborative project initiated by von Trier's email to Leth of 28 November 2000:

> We will watch the movie together and talk about it – then I will set up limitations, commands or prohibitions, which means you have to do the film all over again. This we will do five times – of this the title. I would find it natural if our conversations became a part of the final movie – with the six small films, of course. (Danish Film Institute 2002: 31)

The case for a strong contextualist thesis is easiest to make with regard to *#2: Bombay*. It is one thing for Leth courageously to take up von Trier's challenge and with some reluctance accept the task of staging the formal dinner in a setting of abject poverty and exploitation; it would be something different, and arguably far worse, had he spontaneously taken the initiative to film a staging of a whimsical ceremony of irrelevant gestures and bourgeois dining in such a context.

In the context established by the story of von Trier's challenge, Leth is on record as saying that von Trier has excessively 'Romantic' ideas about the fragility of the observer/participant distinction; Leth tells us that von Trier seems to believe that Leth's habitual stance as a detached observer can somehow be broken down by putting Leth in an uncomfortable situation. Leth denies this and maintains that he can hardly cease to be an outsider and an observer in the red light district of Bombay. This does not mean that he has no strong feelings about the abjection and misery to be observed in this place; in fact he speaks quite eloquently of the horror it represented to him. In accepting von Trier's challenge, Leth has the occasion to comment upon and manifest his opposition to von Trier's supposedly 'Romantic' ideas about the fragility of the observer/participant distinction.

In the imagined, avant-garde context where the idea of staging the scene in this place would have been entirely Leth's own doing, such a

Leth's discomfort

decision would constitute either a repugnant statement of the formalist's die-hard indifference to art's ethical dimensions, or, at best, a belated and shallow attempt to make some kind of politically correct statement about the gap between wealth and poverty. When Leth sings 'Why is happiness so fickle?' in the latter context, the effect is outrageous: is any genuine political insight delivered by the spectacle of a man in a tuxedo having an expensive meal surrounded by misery and exploitation, a man who entertains himself by humming an old-fashioned love song? Such an exercise is more pathetic than probing. In the context of *The Five Obstructions*, however, this moment is part of Leth going through the motions as required by von Trier. Leth's affect is held in check but subtly discernible in his visible discomfort. The strong contextualist thesis also holds with regard to the other embedded films or 'Obstructions'. Consider the following contrasts in relation to *#1: Cuba*.

In The Five Obstructions	In Leth's avant-garde cinema
Rapid editing is a clever response to an externally imposed and perfectly arbitrary rule.	Rapid cutting is an irritating and under-motivated pattern that has been seen too often in avant-garde film.
Looped or repeated shots constitute an ingenious way of obeying the rule while thwarting its limitations, allowing rhythmic editing with short and 'longer' shots constructed through iteration of relatively static shots not longer than 12 frames.	Gimmicky. If the filmmaker wants to use some longer shots to generate rhythm and to allow the observation of some apparently longer gestures, why imitate such shots through iterative construction alone?
Blatant use of stereotypical Cuban imagery (Castro, Che) and props (cigars) count as a flaunting of an arbitrarily imposed geographical and cultural location. The polemical point: you want Cuba, so here is Cuba, at least as it appears to be for those who, like von Trier, have never been there and know nothing about it.	Touristic guide-book and cliché imagery on the theme of Cuba stand in contrast to the modernist brief of a clear and 'objective' observation of subjects. Why Cuba? If Leth's thesis is that human 'perfection' is not a universal essence, but a culturally determined norm, why such a superficial or ironic take on the Cuban context?

The response to the question: 'Why does he move this way?' is a comical flaunting of Trier's injunction to answer the questions raised by the narrator of *The Perfect Human*; the proposed answer ('Because women like it') does not really answer the question, while seeming to do so in a blunt way; all the other questions remain wilfully unanswered in the remake, which reinforces the thought that Leth has cleverly slipped past this obstruction.

The crude, reductive answer to the question is either facilely ironic or stupid; either way, it lends no great thematic depth to the film. Why deviate from the elliptical quality of the original narration by deviating from its ambiguous and deliberate hesitation between an objective, observational stance ('We shall investigate', etc.) and Duchampian whimsy? Why purport to answer the question? There is no good reason.

Readers may disagree with some of these descriptions, or find my emphasis on the contextual contrast hyperbolic. Yet what the reader should be persuaded of is that we cannot come up with a single, plausible description of the audio-visual sequence of *#1: Cuba* that captures its artistic qualities in both of the contexts evoked above. One reason why this is the case is that features of the cinematic design are linked implicitly to the filmmaker's choices, and in the two contexts the choices simply could not be the same: in one context, Leth's choices are influenced directly by von Trier's actions, whereas in the other, they are not. As the strong contextualist thesis would have it, in the context of *The Five Obstructions*, Leth's choices have superior artistic motivation.

To provide a more comprehensive perspective on the strong contextualist thesis, it may be helpful to consider the following questions: how does one 'help' a mature, fiercely independent, avant-garde artist in a context where the 'system' of recognition and rewards places the greatest weight on creative individuality, independence, originality and innovation? How, in such a context, can a younger, more successful and more internationally renowned artist 'help' another artist? And how could the internationally successful director of a series of emotionally engaging (and even melodramatic) fiction films help get a broad audience to see and appreciate the typically non-narrative, modernist filmic experimentations of a relatively obscure Danish director, a figure whose main stylistic antecedents are Jean-Luc Godard and Jean Rouch? Not, presumably, by taking him in tow and incorporating his efforts in a project that would lead to a temporary assimilation or fusion of artistic identities and styles. Nor by giving up the emotional appeal of fictional stories in order to explore the arduous paths of ethnographic non-fictional cinema. Nor by making a backward looking, reverential 'puff' of the older artist's previous works, as in an unlikely and deadly sincere 'homage à Leth' directed by Lars von Trier. The reader will, I hope, have trouble even beginning to imagine von Trier making any such thing. As Mette Hjort (2006) has usefully emphasised, von Trier's 'ingenious devices' of gift-giving are not so obvious and direct.

Viewed in the context of such questions, one can see that von Trier's devious challenge to Leth is the leading edge of a project perfectly designed to respond to this problem. Von Trier will present himself as von Trier while taking on the role of 'Obstructor' (as the credits for 'The Conversations' given at the end of *The Five Obstructions* indicate); in this role he will challenge Leth – identified in these same credits as The Director – and say that he wants to 'banalise' the older artist. The best version of the film is the original one, von Trier *qua* Obstructor proclaims; what he wants to do is to get it ruined [få den ødelagt – the construction used here is a common one for any sort of service one wants to get done, like getting one's shoes polished]. The Obstructor's stated goal in all this has nothing to do with enhancing the artistic value of Leth's work: he says he assumes that the original film, *The Perfect Human*, is the best and it could therefore hardly be his goal to try to get Leth to make something better. In other words, the hopeless 'remake' project on which Leth is to be launched can only give rise to versions that fare poorly by comparison. Yet the Obstructor talks as though this would somehow be good for Leth; the Obstructor's stated goal in getting Leth to accept this self-defeating task is 'therapeutic'.

Under the guise of therapy, then, Leth is given a series of constraints which, though presented as artistically severe and difficult, are in fact a series of moves that contribute to the construction of a highly viable context of artistic creation for Leth. One way of saying just why this context is viable is to follow Jon Elster (2000) in exploring the functional relations between constraints and creativity (see Hjort 2003). There is plenty of evidence in the film to support this idea. At one point in the conversations, Leth explicitly endorses the idea that creativity cannot be purely voluntary or a matter of conscious control; one can, however, indirectly influence one's own involuntary creativity by setting up a 'sluice' or arrangement that can be expected to have the desired result of giving rise to inspiration. Von Trier credits Leth with having introduced the idea of artistic 'rules of the game' into his 'universe'; he is now simply re-applying that helpful lesson to his teacher.

It is also important to observe that the project with its collaboration and constraints also establishes a favourable context of reception, since the viewer's awareness of the external constraints sets parameters for the evaluation of the results. We are not supposed to blame Leth for what would otherwise have to be identified as a highly self-indulgent decision to set himself the task of producing remakes of his late-1960s Godardian short. It is one thing for him to respond to von Trier's odd challenge to produce new versions of the film; it is something else for an artist to decide that a 13-minute film he made some 33 years earlier is the worthy subject for a series of new versions (or even less cogently, 'remakes': one film can obviously provide inspiration or material for a new film, but once a film has been completed it cannot literally be remade).

Authorship and collaboration

The contextualist contrast I have explored above also extends to those aspects of the films affected by questions of authorship. In the context of *The Five Obstructions*, Leth is presented as a filmmaker who tends quite spontaneously not only to work with others but to give his collaborators credit where credit is due. For example, he is quick to tell von Trier *qua* Obstructor that he was glad to adopt Dan Holmberg's genial idea to use a translucent screen as the backdrop of *#2: Bombay*. Leth is shown talking about his exchanges with Bob Sabiston and is presented as seeking out his help with the task of making an animated or 'cartoon' version of *The Perfect Human*. We are shown some of Leth and Sabiston's collaborative encounters where Leth makes a selection from amongst the images Sabiston has generated using motifs from *The Perfect Human* and some of Leth's other films. Leth repeatedly speaks in the first-person plural, referring to his team of collaborators, including his son Asger, who co-authored some of the scripts for the new versions. In sharp contrast to these facts, the Obstructor seems blithely indifferent to any and all questions of collaboration and systematically acts as though the films were the work of Leth alone. His premise would seem to be the Romantic one that the work of art is entirely the manifestation of a single creator's personality; as such, art-making can be part of some one-on-one psycho-therapeutic exercise.

If, on the other hand, we imagine the obstructions in the avant-garde context where they are presented without the conversations and other contextualising materials, Leth would be the one to run the risk of being deemed guilty of burying facts about collaboration and joint authorship in the credits. For example, in *The Five Obstructions* Leth is told to make a cartoon as a kind of punishment for having failed to observe the letter of the Obstructor's law. Leth finds this assignment a severe burden at first, but has the resourcefulness to explore a collaborative solution. The Obstructor has to admit that *#4: Cartoon* is amusing and clever. If we relocate *#4: Cartoon* in the more autonomous context of Leth's own avant-garde initiatives, the work manifests the deceptive artistic feature of an auteur's strangely inauthentic exercise in animation: he seems to have taken up the challenge of making a pastiche of some of his earlier works in an animated medium, but oddly, he does so without also taking up the challenge of actually learning how to work with digital animation. Instead, he gets someone else to do that part and sits back and selects the bits that he likes most. The spectator is not shown this, however, and can only find out about the collaboration by carefully reading the credits, where we find: 'Animation Produced by Flat Black Films, Austin, Texas'.

The fact of the matter is, of course, that we become acquainted with Leth's new versions of *The Perfect Human* in a context in which they are presented as films emerging in response to von Trier's challenges. And in the context of the story presented by *The Five Obstructions*, it is apparent that Leth and his collaborators have made some marvellous short films under difficult circumstances. The ancillary (and I think deceptive and misleading) conclusion to be drawn is that von Trier has failed because he has not realised the kind of 'therapeutic' project he evokes earlier on in the film. My point is that von Trier has not, in fact, failed because psycho-therapy in a strict sense was not the main point of the project.

It might be objected here that the therapeutic project is a key motif in the text that von Trier has Leth read in *#5: Avedøre*. Yet one can respond that the great irony here is that much of this text is a smokescreen. We know that these words are not Leth's; it is also quite likely that they hardly amount to an unmasked and sincere statement of von Trier's thoughts and intentions in this affair. To be sure, the Obstructor does make Leth his *porte-parole* and fallaciously nominates him as The Director of *#5: Avedøre*, but we would do best to classify this as a kind of fiction. In the alternative version of *#5: Avedøre* included as an extra feature on the DVD, von Trier and Leth are shown discussing the comic qualities of the version of *#5: Avedøre* shown in *The Five Obstructions*. Von Trier complains that his text does not hold together or go anywhere, but has to admit that it has an engaging, comic quality, especially when appreciated in relation to the illustrative images. The play of roles within roles has genuine ironic complexity: this is what von Trier would have Leth say if Leth were going to try, unsuccessfully, to unmask von Trier; more pointedly, this is what von Trier would have Leth say as a ruse designed to keep the Obstructor's mask in place. We should remember, here, the tasks von Trier has effectively taken on: to help an avant-garde filmmaker in a context where individuality and originality are crucial desiderata; and to make an excellent collaborative film without betraying the artistic integrity of two very different cinematic authors.

That said so far has taken for granted the assumptions that Leth should be credited as the sole author of the four (or five?) nested new versions, and that von Trier and Leth should be recognised as the joint authors of the nesting or matrix film. Such assumptions are clearly supported by the films' credits, yet they nonetheless require some arguing and elucidation.

Consider, for example, the following paradoxical argument, the foibles of which will be discussed below:

1. Jørgen Leth is the sole author and director of *#1: Cuba* / basis: the credits of *The Five Obstructions*;
2. *#1: Cuba* is part of *The Five Obstructions* / basis: common sense: if

you have not seen this bit you have not seen the entire film; but that condition would obtain only if this bit is part of the film;

3. *The Five Obstructions* was co-directed and co-authored by Leth and von Trier / information given in the credits;

4. The co-directors of a film are its co-authors / this a highly prevalent assumption: who else would be the authors?

5. If someone is the author of a work, that person is the author of any proper part of that work / common sense: if you made a cake, you made the parts of the cake;

6. *#1: Cuba* was co-directed and co-authored by Leth and von Trier / credits, common sense;

7. If a film has co-authors, it cannot have been individually authored by just one person / common sense;

8. Jørgen Leth is not the sole author and director of *#1: Cuba* / this conclusion follows from points 2–7.

This argument is paradoxical. Steps 1–7 are all assumptions that seem correct. The conclusion, 8, follows validly from steps 2–7, but stands in direct contradiction to 1. Something has to be wrong here. The challenge is to identify the misstep, so let us see how that might be done.

There is a misleading tendency to think that authorship only takes place when very special conditions are satisfied (as in a romantic ideal of individual genius and inspiration; for background, see Livingston 2005: chapter 3). Applied to film, this tendency leads to a false choice: on the one hand we have the option of unrealistic Auteur Theory in which we erect a pantheon of real or imagined individual authors in a context where collaboration is the rule, and genuine, individual authorship the exception. On the other hand we give up on authorship and sing in praise of the spontaneously emergent 'text'. Yet this false choice can be avoided if we have a more modest and realistic conception of authorship. It also helps if we recognise that there is such a thing as joint or collaborative authorship, which can be contrasted not only to individual authorship but to cases where the making of an artefact really is a chaotic and uncoordinated collection of doings and events. The important, but difficult, question, then, is this: under what conditions do two or more persons count as joint authors of a work?

Two basic elements must, I think, be combined if we are to succeed in articulating those conditions. The first element pertains to the kinds of expressive actions that have to be performed if one is to be an author of any sort at all; the second element pertains to the type of coordination that must obtain if actions of this sort performed by more than one person are to count as joint expressive actions.

First of all, authorship requires some kind of (relatively) uncoerced expressive action. It does not have to be original, innovative or of any high quality. There is bad, trite and routine authorship. There may be a place for an honorific notion of Author, but first we need to identify a purely classificatory conception. Relatively 'uncoerced' means no one is using severe threats to force the party in question to do something. Coercion is a matter of degree, especially if we think about the more subtle sorts of economic coercion to which most people are subject throughout their lives. The kind of extreme coercion in which authorship is totally vitiated is best exemplified by cases where dictators, a band of criminals or terrorists force someone to make a statement or even a feature-length film (as was the case with Barbet Schroeder's *General Idi Amin Dada* (1976)).

By 'expressive action', I mean any activities that serve to indicate someone's attitudes (be those attitudes genuine or feigned; see Davis 1988). When Leth and von Trier appear on film each saying in turn 'I hate cartoons', they each express the corresponding attitude in the sense that they give the spectator some (possibly misleading) indication or evidence to the effect that they hate cartoons. Someone who neither makes nor displays anything indicative of any attitudes cannot be an author; anyone who does engage in such expressive actions is in a broad sense an author. Authorship is not, then, a razor sharp concept: coercion is a matter of degree, and so is the making of utterances. Someone who scratches his head in puzzlement has thereby expressed an attitude, but whether this gesture counts as an utterance constitutive of authorship or not is probably not worth going into. No such vagueness pertains, however, to a carefully crafted 13-minute avant-garde film.

How this 'uncoerced expression' condition is to be extended to cases where more than one person is involved is not as straightforward a matter as one might wish. The simple solution would be to say that two persons are joint authors of a given utterance to the extent that the utterance is the intentional expression of attitudes they hold in common. It would follow, of course, that the joint authors must not have been coerced by other parties, but also that neither of them has coerced the other. In a situation where several people collaborate on a work but only one of them has the power to make all of the final decisions and systematically coerces the other parties into complying with his or her dictates, only the latter person could be counted as the author of the work. But if the two or more parties intentionally work together to make an utterance that expresses their commonly held attitudes (sincerely or not), this is a case of joint authorship.

There is a problem, however, with the straightforward assumption that two or more persons can only co-author a work if it is presented as representing only attitudes they share. That is why we also need an additional condition pertaining to the kind of coordination that obtains in instances of joint authorship. In some cases, collaborators design a work to indicate and make public attitudes about which they disagree as well as points they hold in common. Books organised as a dialogue or debate between two or more parties are a familiar example. We can say that such authors co-authored the book, even if it is also clear that only a particular individual author expresses his or her opinion in some segment of the work. The work as a whole is jointly authored by contributors X, Y and Z whereas X writes one part, Y another part and Z yet another, assuming, that is, that there was some kind of intentional cooperation in the organisation and combination of these individual efforts.

One way to couch this last condition is to follow Michael E. Bratman (1999) in speaking of 'meshing sub-plans' as a requirement on collective agency. John's plan is to refute Jacques' every argument, and vice versa, which means both plans cannot be realised by the same book; yet their respective sub-plans or means to that end – the publication of a book representing their debate – are structurally identical, compatible and can be simultaneously acted on and realised. These shared and reciprocally known plans allow them to work together and function more or less smoothly as joint authors.

For example, von Trier contacts Leth by email and proposes that they make a film together based on a given scheme, the details of which remain to be worked out. The scheme allows for and even encourages certain elements of competition, negotiation and conflict, yet like the rules of a competitive game, the scheme is a shared plan of action that permits both rivalrous and cooperative moves. Neither party will have the power or motivation needed to coerce the other party into doing anything as they act on their shared scheme, but it is not part of their plan to display the result as expressing only attitudes they hold in common. It is, however, perfectly correct to say that the resulting work or utterance is co-authored by these two collaborating filmmakers.

We will probably never know how much genuine competition was in play in Leth's and von Trier's interactions in the making of *The Five Obstructions*. Whether the film can be resolutely classified as fiction or non-fiction is far from obvious, but even if one tends to think that it was on the whole framed by its makers as targeting belief rather than make-believe or imaginings, it has to be recognised that fictionalising was a means along the way, if not the ultimate end. Although the credits do not include the usual 'work of fiction' disclaimer, they do list von Trier as a performer playing the role of 'Obstructor' and Leth that of 'Director'. My own inclination is to credit Leth and von Trier as joint authors of a film that is meant to balance precariously at the border of fiction and non-fiction.

How do these considerations about authorship help us with the paradoxical argument introduced above? I do not think we want to deny that Leth is the author of *#1: Cuba*. Although it is obvious that he has collaborated with many people in the making of this short film, the assumption is that he was the ultimate decision-maker and the film is presented as expressing his accomplishment and attitudes. So step 1 in the argument is sound. Yet Leth is also one of the two co-authors of *The Five Obstructions*. Unless some of the other steps in the argument are erroneous, we are drawn back in the direction of the paradoxical conclusion that Leth both is and is not the sole author of *#1: Cuba* and the other new versions.

The error in the paradoxical argument can, however, be identified and avoided. It is a matter of equivocation around the word 'author', as one is not the individual author of a nested part of a work in the same sense that one is a co-author or joint author of the work as a whole. Step 5 in the argument, which is presented as being supported by common sense, is the culprit: someone can be one of the co-authors of a collective work without being the author, at least *in the same sense*, of all of its parts. For the sake of comparison, consider the idea that if one participates in a presidential election and votes against an ultimately victorious George W. Bush, one has elected Bush in the sense that one voted for Bush. This is obviously a fallacious inference. There are some kinds of collective actions where a part-whole inference of this sort is valid, but there are other sorts of joint activities where it is not, and my claim here is that authorship (at least of certain types of works) is one of them.

Conclusion

Nesting is a very prevalent representational device and its functions in the arts are multifarious. In some contexts, nesting serves as a kind of meta-fictional pointer that highlights the artificial or constructed nature of a representation. In other contexts, however, nesting contributes to the project of telling a plausible or even truthful story about artists or filmmakers. I have suggested that in the case of *The Five Obstructions*, the nesting of works by Leth and his collaborators has the function of constituting a favourable context for both the making and reception of Leth's cinematic art. Although Leth's avant-garde or experimental films have long been admired by *cognoscenti*, the context that *The Five Obstructions* establishes allows a wider audience to appreciate the skill with which Leth and his collaborators successfully respond to von Trier's challenges. Obviously, the challenges themselves provide Leth with help in the form of motivation and orientation, but my point here has also been that the film's skilfully crafted story of the Leth/von Trier interaction constitutes a favourable context for the reception and appreciation of the nested works, which acquire certain positively valenced stylistic and thematic qualities only in this context. And this is partly what makes Lars von Trier's 'Help Jørgen Leth' project a success.[1]

NOTE

1 The work described in this chapter was partially supported by a grant from the Research Grants Council of the Hong Kong Special Administrative Region, China (Project No. LU3401/06H). I am very grateful for this support. I would also like to thank Sondra Bacharach and Mette Hjort for helpful comments on an early draft.

WORKS CITED

Borges, Jorge Luis (1998 [1939]) 'Pierre Menard, Author of the *Quixote*', trans. Andrew Hurley, in Jorge Luis Borges, *Collected Fictions*. New York: Viking, 88–95.

Bratman, Michael E. (1999) *Faces of Intention: Selected Essays on Intention and Agency*. Cambridge: Cambridge University Press.

Danish Film Institute (2002) *Film: Special Issue/Leth*. Copenhagen: Danish Film Institute.

Danto, Arthur (1981) *The Transfiguration of the Commonplace*. Cambridge, MA: Harvard University Press.

Davis, Wayne A. (1988) 'Expression of Emotion', *American Philosophical Quarterly*, 25, 279–91.

Elster, Jon (2000) *Ulysses Unbound: Studies in Rationality, Precommitment, and Constraints*. Cambridge: Cambridge University Press.

Hjort, Mette (2003) 'Dogma '95: A Small Nation's Response to Globalisation', in Mette Hjort and Scott MacKenzie (eds) *Purity and Provocation: Dogma 95*. London: British Film Institute, 31–47.

_____ (2006) 'Gifts, Games, and Cheek: Counter-Globalisation in a Privileged Small-Nation Context: The Case of *The Five Obstructions*', in Claire Thomsen (ed.) *Northern Constellations: New Readings in Nordic Cinema*. Norwich: Norvik Press, 41–59.

Levinson, Jerrold (1990) 'Titles', in *Music, Art, and Metaphysics*. Ithaca: Cornell University Press, 159–78.

Livingston, Paisley (2003) 'Nested Art', *Journal of Aesthetics and Art Criticism*, 61, 233–45.

_____ (2005) *Art and Intention*. Oxford: Clarendon Press.

Walton, Kendall L. (1970) 'Categories of Art', *Philosophical Review*, 79, 334–67.

Wollheim, Richard (1978) 'Are the Criteria of Identity that Hold for a Work of Art in the Different Arts Aesthetically Relevant?', *Ratio*, 20, 29–48.

Work and Play: The 5-O Game

TREVOR PONECH

The Five Obstructions, as I understand it, is well described as an asymmetrically-played agonistic game. The name of the 5-O game is, of course, 'let's make a movie'. But its particular nature and dynamics derive from an underlying cluster of precepts recognisable to viewers of a certain variety of documentary film. These precepts consist of precommitments to participation, provocation and truth-seeking by means of cinematic artifice and imagination. Hence, the 5-O game is played in the spirit of *cinémavérité*. Indeed game leader Lars von Trier's quasi-therapeutic ulterior motives – provocation of illuminating, potentially transformative psychosocial truths from its players – are iterations, with an infusion of mordant asceticism, of those motivating such a classic *vérité* work as *Chronicle of a Summer* (*Chronique d'un été*, Jean Rouch and Edgar Morin, 1960).

The Five Obstructions does not only, or mainly, document a game. To state my thesis in a stronger voice: *The Five Obstructions* is the game. Adding a stitch to my argument, I propose that *The Five Obstructions* is something properly called a 'cinematic work'. And in this case, that work comprises a course of actions and achievements properly called a game.

Given its centrality, the concept of 'game' deserves attention at the outset. The word's inscrutability equals its familiarity. Consider the vast, multifarious array of things thereunder grouped. We wonder what, if any, uniformity makes poker, dungeons and dragons, soccer, roulette, skiing, kite-flying, mud pies, spin-the-bottle, practical jokes, avoiding sidewalk cracks and searching clouds for animal shapes members of the same kind. Maybe that relationship is no more than family resemblance, each member having some feature belonging to another, but none sharing any single definitive feature with all others (see Wittgenstein 1968: 66–7). To accept this premise is to abandon prematurely the search for the deep story about games.

Better to cast our lot with Roger Caillois. Though hardly incontrovertible, his analysis promises insight into the psychological, social and experiential dimensions of a quintessentially human phenomenon. He starts from the premise that games are forms of play. Thus he establishes a common thread between outwardly dissimilar things in these being expressions of the same basic activity. What, then, is play? Caillois defines it as behaviour that is essentially free, separate, uncertain, unproductive and rule-governed or make-believe (1961: 9–10). It comes in four basic kinds: *agôn*, or competitive play; *alea*, that is, games of chance; mimicry, which involves simulation and acting 'as if'; and games of *ilinx*, vertigo-inducing, tumultuous play. Caillois argues that any game or episode of play can be further described in relation to its position along a spectrum ranging from *paidia* to *ludus*. With *paidia*, he means exuberant, impulsive, improvisational, sometimes delirious play of the sort associated with childhood. *Ludus* designates instances of play decisively shaped by reason and culture – contrived and calculated, institutionalised and rule-bound even to the point of 'gratuitous difficulty' (1961: 27). Along the spectrum towards *ludus*, play is increasingly trammelled by deliberations about how best to perform the activity, by technique, skill, rule formulation and following, by the use of props and equipment. Graduation towards the ludic, says Caillois, sees the emergence of those activities stereotypically considered games as such (1961: 29).

That play is free, voluntary action is apparent. Forced at gunpoint into a Scrabble match, my wordsmithery is but joyless rule following; internally compelled, obsessive Scrabble-playing does not sound very playful, either. Uncertainty is also a good candidate for a defining property, to the extent that play unfolding programmatically towards foregone conclusions most likely only amuses the neophyte participant. The putative contributions of rules and make-believe to the nature of play are harder to grasp. Caillois supposes this pair to be opposed and mutually exclusive: 'games are not ruled and make-believe. Rather, they are ruled or make-believe' (1961: 9). These play principles are nevertheless functionally equivalent. Both create what Caillois terms a 'fiction'. Playing at cops and robbers or pretending to be an airplane, your game revolves around imitating something that really exists – something that you in reality are not. Playing chess or tennis, you likewise escape reality, only in a different way. The rules according to which you act are unreal because they have no correspondence with or application to ordinary life, which revolves around meeting responsibilities and doing productive work. A game's rules exist only for their own sake, are meaningless, since no one is ultimately obliged to follow them and they serve to produce nothing but the game.

Caillois evidently holds rules to be culturally ossified instances of a more general phenomenon, regulation (1961: 28–9). This latter encompasses everything from technique and specialised skills, to utensils, to the sorts of mental and motor capacities for self-control one exerts when frightening one's self with scary thoughts or guiding one's bodily movements during leapfrog. But what differentiates a rule from a regulation, and why rules, though presumably not regulation, are incompatible with make-believe remain unclear. Without that cogency, it's not obvious that all play must be either rule-governed or make-believe. Skipping stones over water is neither, even if it does presuppose motor-control and the laws of physics. Likewise for such *ilinx* hijinks as twirling until dizzy. And in lots of play, especially of the 'as if' variety, it is impossible to detach make-believe from ruliness. Think of a game of cops and robbers, which requires participants to entertain in imagination ad hoc stipulations like, 'I'm a detective this time' and 'let those bricks be gold bars'.

The concepts of separateness and unproductivity also make trouble. Play, the space in which it occurs, and the time of its occurrence are supposedly out of joint with ordinary life. Caillois variously invokes an 'imaginary milieu', a 'suspension of reality' and 'the creation of a fictional world' (1961: 19, 22, 135); vertigo, he says, 'destroys reality' via motor-perceptual and cognitive discombobulation (1961: 23). Play and games surely have an intelligible difference from other kinds of human actions and experiences. But we need no special metaphysics to grasp their nature. In ontological strictness, the game board and gridiron, the disequilibrated perception, and the episode of imaginative make-believe exist at no remove, much less an 'absolute' one (1961: 45), from physical, spatio-temporal, social and psychoperceptual reality. Nor is play distinguished from other activities by unproductivity. Caillois' thinking is that play occasions 'pure waste' ('la dépense pure'), for example of time, energy, abilities, money and so forth (1961: 5–6). Even when, as in gambling games, participants could gain financially, play is waste because nothing is harvested or made, no capital increased. Property or money might be exchanged, but no goods or wealth generated. Caillois is gripped by the idea that play is the inefficient efflux of trans-species 'surplus vital energy' deflecting human behaviour from modern society's utilitarian, means-ends rational order (1961: 163). This leads him to inflate play's noninstrumentality and unproductivity. Play is valuable precisely because of ends it enables us to realise. Some consist of pleasurable experiences – sensory-motor, cognitive, imaginative, emotional, social – it affords. Others comprise achievements. Players sometimes manage feats of skill, ingenuity, creativity, imagination, wit, grace and beauty, the prospect of such accomplishments helping to make the game worth playing.

A revised working definition of games retains the insight that they are modes of play, that is, activity entered into freely and with uncertainty as to how exactly it will end. It goes on to propose that play needn't be either make-believe or rule-bound but that games *per se*, whether or not they involve pretence, are regulated play. Here the sense of 'regulated' extends from the formal, institutionalised ruliness of, say, basketball to the local, contextual stipulations people sometimes invent as facilitating constraints on their play. Though neither ontologically autonomous nor discontinuous from reality and the flow of ordinary life, play does tend to be quarantined. 'Bricks are gold bars' is not true *simpliciter*; it's only true in the make-believe of our current cops and robbers game, in which we knowingly, without illusion, adopt a prescription to think of bricks as gold bars. That a player three or more feet from the ball can be penalised for an obstruction if he screens an opponent from it is not an effective condition on how one acts off the soccer pitch. Similarly, games normally have finite though not necessarily inflexible spatial and/or temporal boundaries that shape and facilitate play. In some games, like fencing, protective equipment and prohibitions against roughness impose a bulwark against injurious aggression. In all four examples, the quarantining of play turns on its pragmatic – a cognitive and practical – separation from other activities and spheres of life, not an ontological one. The function is to facilitate play and enable participants to focus on and enjoy its constitutive activities in their own right.

Caillois remarks, 'Play is an end in itself' (1961: 167). Let us sharpen this idea by describing play as inherently valuable activity. I agree that inherent is a variety of instrumental value (see Lewis 1946; Stecker 1997; Livingston 2004). Something's inherent value is its power, under certain conditions, to produce an intrinsically valued experience. Such an experience is good in itself – or is at least felt to be so by some individual. Play is paradigmatic of an inherently valuable activity. Whatever else motivates your participation, for an activity to count as play it must offer you a distinctive, absorbing experience that is itself a final, if not exclusive, end. The experience's intrinsic value is registered affectively, by pleasure you (expect to) take in it. When you play, you act in anticipation of an enjoyable experience of, for instance, competition, chance, pretence, vertigo or some other kind of inherently valued activity – including imagination, to which pretence might be reduced, and *eros*. A play activity's capacity to realise such an experience, or combination thereof, is its inherent, likely predominant, value for you.

In the absence of an exhaustive definition of play and games, the foregoing heuristic narrows the scope of these concepts without arbitrarily diminishing the phenomenal diversity associated with them. A case in point is the sentiment that movie-making can be a sort of game. This claim is often casually made in reference to various major directors, such as Orson Welles and Alfred Hitchcock; Lars von Trier, too, has been said to take a ludic approach to filmmaking (Schepelern 2003: 58). Whether movie-making is ever really at all like game-play, and what interpretive significance this analogy might have, are open questions – ones best posed in relation to actual episodes of movie-making. *The Five Obstructions*, then, is an opportunity to test our intuitions.

The Five Obstruction's production sure looks like a game. The affair begins with von Trier's challenge, sent by email to Leth: do over your short film *The Perfect Human* five times, according to my 'limitations, commands or prohibitions' (Danish Film Institute 2002: 31). We will meet, he says, to discuss each new version; these conversations will be part of the final film in which the remakes are presented. The challenger proceeds to speculate over how to maximise their 'fun' by seeking ways to ensure big differences between the original and the five new works. In an email reply, Leth accepts the dare, thinking it 'exciting' and finding appeal in the challenge of adapting on the fly to unforeseen, adventitious obstacles (ibid.).

Von Trier dubs his challenge 'the five obstructions', a sporting metaphor foreshadowing parlous play. In soccer, obstructions – *benspænd* – occur when players block, grab or trip one another. By the same token, it's apparent the 5-O game, assuming it is a game, is an agonistic one. Von Trier and Leth are to be competitors; the object of their rivalry is Leth's personal and artistic autonomy. A von Trier victory depends on preventing his opponent from making movies not distinctively Leth's own, on compelling him to work in ways that flout his ingrained preferences. Leth favours long takes; the Obstructor's first commandment is to make a film comprising shots of no more than 12 frames. During their next meeting, von Trier announces his desire to 'banalise' Leth. This time, he shall directly attack the impersonalness and composure of his work. If the original film *The Perfect Human* exemplifies the distance Leth affects from the things he describes, then the second obstruction will force a display of 'empathy' from Leth: he shall pretend to be the Perfect Man, the camera focused upon him as he dines alone at a banquet set amidst real but unseen human suffering. A subsequent constraint requires Leth to make a cartoon, a form he rejects as inimical to his belief in waiting and observing as the unforeseen or uncontrollable transpires before the lens.

The two men are well matched as expert cinematic practitioners whose clash of experience, skills and cunning makes the contest's path and ultimate outcome anything but predictable. Yet, if not skewed to either's advantage, the 5-O game is strikingly asymmetrical. The difference is reflected in their prescribed roles. Though also putting himself on exhibition, von Trier is aptly characterised as the observer, Leth as his subject. After all, the game is contrived to examine the responses of this Perfect Human who, as von Trier recalls during a monologue, introduced the young von Trier to the idea of filmmaking as a rule-governed enterprise. Now von Trier gives Leth the rule. Sporting analogies aside, 5-O is also a version of Simon Says, the game leader's instructions designed to confuse or unbalance the follower. Von Trier the taskmaster is bent on felling Leth, by inducing the 'moral' *ilinx* of psychological disorder (see Caillois 1961: 24).

Von Trier's commandments generally appear to be extemporaneous, improvisational creations: Leth's stated preference for precise framing in which uncontrollable events might unfold evidently inspires von Trier, moments later in their conversation, to foist upon him a cartoon. However, 5-O is not without a bedrock of relatively more formal, *a priori* regulatory principles. Specifically, the game's premises are iterations of a trio of documentary filmmaking precepts associated with a particular strain of *cinéma-vérité*. Foremost is a commitment to participation.

Cinéma-vérité from its inception rejected the stolid rituals of television news and the impersonal empiricism of Griersonian social documentaries and traditional ethnographic films. Its proponents conceived it as plunging the filmmaker into real people's lives and real-life interpersonal relations (see Morin 2003: 229–32). Taking that plunge invites complicity. Consider Rouch and Morin's *Chronicle of a Summer* which assembles a cast of Parisians – men, women, office workers, labourers, intellectuals, merchants, students – around the project of interrogating whether they are happy with their lives. Rather than being objects of unobtrusive observation, cast members conspire with the filmmakers to stage various interviews, arguments and social exchanges – between themselves, with Rouch and Morin, with strangers – in their homes, places of work and out in the street. Finally they are shown viewing a rough cut then critiquing the project's goals, the perspicuity of the unfinished film's representations, and the authenticity of their own and others' on- and off-screen personae.

Apart from inviting their subjects' complicity, one of the co-authors' key decisions is to 'mingle' with their characters (Morin 2003: 233).

Rouch and Morin, too, are the film's subjects. They intend their work to be partly about their interactions with the cast and each other, their experience of making the film, and own response to it. Their authorial self-observation culminates in an *autocritique* after the rough cut's screening. Walking along the hall of the Musée de l'Homme, they ponder cast members' reproving, unsympathetic mutual accusations of exhibitionism and inauthenticity. Rather than raising individuals' social masks or removing artificial barriers to empathy and recognition of shared humanity, the filmmakers suspect their cinematic experiment of generating new masks and barriers. 'Nous sommes dans le bain' (literally: 'we are in the bath'), concludes Morin; we are implicated in, mixed up in the project's wayward consequences.

Mingling extends to a further, distinctive mode of participation in characters' lives. Here I single out a second core *cinéma-vérité* policy, namely a commitment to provocation. *Chronicle of a Summer*'s authors are not so much interested in discovering and recording psychosocial dramas as precipitating them. It is axiomatic for Rouch and Morin that it is both possible and desirable for 'the camera' to provoke events, especially otherwise unattainable self-revelations. Equipping her with a small audio recorder, they accompany a central character, Marceline, to Place de la Concorde to film her from a distance walking alone, talking to herself. As she strolls, Marceline recalls her deportation to Auschwitz in an emotional monologue addressed to her father, who perished in the camp. Cut to Les Halles where, still pretending to speak to her father, she evokes the bittersweet postwar reunion of her surviving family on a train platform. Rouch would later describe Marceline's impromptu disclosure of memories and despair as totally artificial and provoked, yet totally sincere (see Levin 1971: 137); and as an unforeseen outcome of an 'intolerable *mise-en-scène*' (Rouch 2003: 153).

Morin, interviewed by a newspaper while editing *Chronicle of a Summer*, comments that what interests him in documentary is not showing 'appearances' but, rather, 'an active intervention to cut across appearances and extract from them their hidden or dormant truths' (2003: 252–3). A third *vérité* precept thus links provocation to truth-seeking, especially where truth pertains to realities of selfhood and personal identity. Yet these human realities, Rouch and Morin's film experiment ultimately suggests, are sometimes the stuff of imagination. Marceline insists that while the memories she recounts in her monologue are genuine, she was nonetheless playacting, dramatising herself in a tragic role of her own spontaneous creation. During their *autocritique*, the co-authors wonder if even Marceline knows whether she was just acting; perhaps the fictional persona she presents betokens a part of her self as authentic as any other she presents to the world. *Cinéma-vérité's* provocations might expose imaginary facets of its participants' selves.

The 5-O game reprises *vérité's* hallmark precepts – more precisely, precommitments – concerning participation, provocation and truth-seeking. Precommitments number among the *a priori*, conditional preferences, plans and policies, schematic or detailed, implicit or explicit, that guide filmmakers in crafting their projects (see Ponech 1999). Think of these mental items as recipes that, once adopted, settle the filmmaker on a few objectives and some practical steps appropriate to achieving them. The kind of work I associate with the *vérité* documentary arises when filmmakers embrace and follow the aforementioned policy triad. Independent of whether either of *The Five Obstructions'* co-authors explicitly understood himself as beholden to *cinéma-vérité's* norms, their cinematic game proceeds accordingly.

When multiple participants are involved, play is collaborative activity. The production of such an escapade, the point of playing and fun of it, are predicated upon complicity, even if the game were agonistic. 5-O conforms to these truisms; it differs from other games in that participation consists of exercising fully blown cinematic agency. Someone is a cinematic agent to the degree that he acts with both the intention and power to make significant, more rather than less effective contributions to the communicative, expressive and aesthetic properties a film has independent of audiences' perceptual and interpretive uptake (see Gaut 1997; Livingston 1997). Being an eager documentary subject or seizing a chance to make a spectacle of one's self do not guarantee cinematic agency. The agent must operate within a particular psychological framework, roughly: a major reason for my embarking on this course of thought and action is my realising a cinematic work or part of it. Moreover, in collaborative filmmaking contexts, cinematic agency necessitates robust coordination. Agents commit to 'mutual responsiveness', to borrow some technical jargon (Bratman 1992: 327). They try to mesh with those of others their own deliberations, plans and efforts regarding content, form, style, and so on, each agent expecting that mutual responsiveness will help complete the project. (In this light, only some of *Chronicle of a Summer*'s subjects, like Marceline, exhibit, beyond complicity, a modicum of cinematic agency.)

The Five Obstructions stands out from other *cinéma-vérité* works in that von Trier's plunge into Leth's existence is a contest between cinematic agents who play by ascribing different, asymmetrical roles to themselves. Von Trier, usurping Leth's normal role, becomes the observer. The participant observer, actually. For von Trier is intent on mingling with his subject. One way he does so is by meshing his diktats into Leth's artistic plans, activities and results. 'Meshing into' captures the *agôn* of their collaboration. Globally, they cooperate by following the rules, sticking to schedules and budgets, exchanging and sharing material resources and personnel, and otherwise sharing the goal of jointly making a movie called *The Five Obstructions*. Thus, the opponents reciprocally help each other play the game. Locally, though, their mutual responsiveness serves combative ends. The Obstructor tries thwarting the Director's ability to make anything but 'crap' by imposing on him constraints negatively attuned to Leth's sensibilities. Von Trier shiftily associates victory with eliciting 'that feeling of a tortoise on its back'. A feeling in Leth, as of being? In von Trier, as of looking at? Leth, too, observes, takes notes – 'Yes. Tortoise. I'll write it down' – and one-ups von Trier by keeping the turtle right side up and mobile. Winning for him is a matter of staying upright, like his 'role model', footballer Michael Laudrup, who 'attracted obstructions … and elegantly always avoided to fall or get injured' (Danish Film Institute 2002: 32). Not falling means drawing fodder for imagination from the obstructions. 'The trouble', complains von Trier, 'is you're so clever that whatever I say inspires you.' 'Yes', Leth responds, 'I can't help it.'

Obstructor is also provocateur. Von Trier's constraints are supposedly catalysts – in his rhetoric of asceticism, 'chastisements', 'flagellations'. I have likened 5-O to Simon Says. Played, I add, as an 'ascetic game' (see

'Yes. Tortoise. I'll write it down'

Caillois 1961: 16).Von Trier challenges Leth to an ordeal of privations and discomfiting situations. He supposes his metaphorical flagellations could trigger a 'scream', a moment of incontinence in which his adversary's inner turmoil is expressed, by channeling Leth into a creative impasse. This bout of psychological vertigo might, he imagines, have a reformative effect on its subject. Hence *The Five Obstructions*' provocations, like those of *Chronicle of a Summer*, have an informally therapeutic aim. Rouch and Morin dive into a plurality of solitudes in a bid to relieve their subjects of repressive, distorting masks and social atomisation.Von Trier partly construes the 5-O game as a means to cure Leth of personally and artistically debilitating inauthenticity.

In *#5: Avedøre*, where Leth becomes his nemesis's *porte-parole*, von Trier charges that Leth's films, like his 'rows of Armani suits', are vehicles of a 'personal fiction'. Since *The Perfect Human* – a pastiche of the ethnographic film – Leth in his cinematic projects has played the role of detached, quizzical observer of an exotic Other, namely, the human. By repetition of his rules, he hides his true self behind an appearance of 'perverse perfection'. But his emotionally disengaged, analytic exercises in observation and description plus the steadiness and composure of his imagery comprise a façade meant to conceal, not least of all from himself, the acute 'angst' and messy 'insecurity' Leth shares with abject humans.

Von Trier plays 5-O according to a quintessentially *vérité* vow he once made 'to force the truth out of my characters and settings' (Von Trier and Vinterberg 2003: 200). More so than *Chronicle of a Summer*, 5-O's method of extracting illuminating personal truths is filmmaking itself. According to Rouch, the camera is for *Chronicle of a Summer*'s participants a 'pretext' (2003: 154); it is also both 'a mirror [and] a window open to the outside' (quoted in Cameron & Shivas 1963: 22). It is a pretext because it helps filmmakers and their accomplices invent novel opportunities for self-revelation. Recall Marceline's stroll: an idiosyncratic situation, including the subjectively felt imperative to perform for the recording devices, prompts her to descend into herself and results in a theatricalised expression of memories and emotions. Participation in the *vérité* film extends to viewing the cinematic representations of one's self, with an eye to critiquing them and those of other participants. The camera is associated with both mirror and window insofar as its use facilitates self-awareness and communication among participants. The 5-O game encompasses these elements; it also goes a step further. Von Trier not only pins his subject beneath the camera's lens so that he might reveal something hidden for all, including the subject, to see; he also makes an expert practitioner struggle with practical and creative problems of filmmaking under barbed constraints customised to chafe, like a bespoke hair shirt.

Von Trier's game, therefore, involves *askesis*, an exercise in submission and denial intended for its subject's putative good. Spurious intimations of the sacred aside, this is secular asceticism aiming at a peculiar sort of psychological health, one conducive to artistic renewal. Trial by barbed obstructions, which includes holding up a mirror to the subject, aims to show him what he really is. This gruelling episode of critical reflection is supposed to motivate Leth to confront and embrace his inner demons, thereby relieving him of his self-deception and psychic estrangement. Unshackled, those demons – the 'beautiful bird' von Trier wishes to 'chase' until it takes wing – might inflect Leth's artistic practices and move him towards making films having the personal presence and authenticity von Trier finds lacking from Leth's work.

Von Trier ultimately posits truths of his own psyche and relation to Leth. *#5: Avedøre* is his self-chastening 'dans le bain' moment of autocritique. He acknowledges constructing a fictive Leth, cut to the measure of his self-serving fantasy that this model of cinematic agency deep down 'is a wretch, just like me'. During this loquacious sequence epitomising Edgar Morin's notion that *cinéma-vérité*'s action is the spoken word (2003: 252), von Trier obliquely confesses his own self-deception: 'You only saw what you wanted to see.' The affected cinematic *Perfekte Menneske* concealing a von Trier-like wretch is a figment of von Trier's own imagination; the vision of a dramatic breakdown followed by the grateful wretch 'staggering out of the ruins', a Romantic conceit. Von Trier apparently realises that, over-valuing 'the scream', he conflates failure to 'let it out' with disavowal of an essential part of any human's 'true self'. It is actually not so obvious which of the conflicting, occlusive, inconsistent parts of Leth's identity constitute his true self. The answer, say some philosophers, is really up to the individual (see Frankfurt 1989). It depends on which of the refractory passions and dispositions arising within him he identifies with – which ones he wholeheartedly wants to have, and to will and act according to. That when he picks up the camera, Leth can't or won't help it but that the scream stays inside and his hands stay steady might indicate Leth is in possession of himself, not that he is trying 'to fool the world'. If von Trier has been 'arrogant', as he has his *porte-parole* describe him, it is by supposing that a spasm of emotion would express, not violate, that which is central to Leth's sense of personal identity.

Readers might by now wonder what point is left in claiming that von Trier and Leth play a game. Play is supposedly an end in itself. Their activities seem tied to more serious business; 5-O is, as Caillois would say, contaminated by reality. Indeed, one bit of business 5-O is tied to is the production of cinematic art. For Caillois, who believes play essentially to be pure waste, their productivity in this regard suffices to rule out saying literally that the two men play a game. 'A characteristic of play', says Caillois, 'is that it creates no wealth or goods, thus differing from work or art' (1961: 5). I disagree. Practical, instrumental and productive ends are hardly inconsistent with game play. The difference between play and non-play is psychological. It turns on participants' attitudes towards and

Von Trier obstructed by the Perfect Human

experiences of their activities. These activities can be highly productive. They can even be works.

Many of our projects and undertakings might qualify as works. But currently I have in mind items – including novels, paintings, musical compositions and performances, and of course films – to which we are inclined to attribute artistic value, owing to their communicative, expressive and aesthetic qualities and powers. Used to describe such things, 'work' refers to both a process and an achievement aspect of cinematic agency. *The Five Obstructions* considered as a work includes the various moves von Trier, Leth and their artistic collaborators execute in the process of making their film. Consider the second set of obstructions. Von Trier's move is at once cogitative and overt. It encompasses the mental act of conceiving the strictures; it extends to the communicative act of telling Leth to choose 'the most miserable place on earth [and] go close to a few really harrowing things … that you refrain from filming'. In turn, Leth's move is to interpret von Trier's constraints. He has the help of cinematographer Dan Holmberg, who has the idea of inserting a diaphanous screen between Leth and the destitute onlookers as the Perfect Man capers and dines in Falkland Road. Their forethought and imagination in reaction to von Trier's commandments, their reconsideration of Leth's initial plan to insert an opaque screen, plus subsequent practical steps they take to get the fruits of their deliberations into the form of projectible images and sounds, all constitute parts of the work as process.

A work's achievement consists of a product. With Holmberg's aid, what Leth manages to produce is an interpretation of the strictures, plus imagery adapted to the job of enabling audiences to grasp it. Leth's achievement, then, is the imaginative use of *mise-en-scène* to play with the obstructions' meaning. The screen suggests the occlusion von Trier demands. At the same time, it suggests the projection, as on a movie screen, of carefully selected and framed images of reality – reality contained and at a remove, relative to the Perfect Man in the foreground. Responding to obstructions meant to strip away the Director's 'highly affected distance' from the world, Leth and Holmberg create a visual metaphor for that distance.

I identify the work *The Five Obstructions* with exercises of cinematic agency and certain of their outcomes. Besides von Trier, Leth and Holmberg, plausible cinematic agents include this film's editors, assistant cinematographer, second unit director, sound designer and various theatrical performers. The range of work-specifying contributions is correspondingly broad and rich. Generally, these are to be sought among episodes of deliberation, reconsideration, imaginative thinking, trial and error experimentation, precommitment, planning and practical action occurring as the aforementioned, mutually responsive individuals carry out their production tasks. These moves and achievements are identical to those comprising what I have dubbed 'the 5-O game'; this and '*The Five Obstructions*' refer to the same one, particular ensemble of moves and achievements, the same one work, like 'Polaris' and 'North Star' refer to the same one, particular celestial body. It is not that one item coexists with the other; or that two things have somehow, like eggs into an omelette, been combined or homogenised. There is but one thing, the cinematic work. The claim, 'This work is a game' is made true by facts about its co-authors' psychological relationship to that work, facts about why they undertake it and what sorts of experiences they associate with it. Like Holmberg, who plays for Leth, other participants might partake of this relation. Those who do not regard themselves as players are, from a certain point of view, also nonetheless game instruments, as they are at the disposal of players von Trier and Leth, who marshal and direct their contributions to the work.

The Five Obstructions does not merely document a game. What's more, the experimental styles and fictional dimensions of the embedded obstruction films stop the work as a whole from fitting the profile of a typical or usual documentary (see Plantinga 2005). Nevertheless, The Five Obstructions is nonfiction. Like Chronicle of a Summer, it is a work committed to truth-seeking and communication between participants. Like Chronicle of a Summer, its route to knowledge of selfhood is cinematic artifice. Von Trier, if not Leth, assumes filmmaking can create a pretext, be a catalyst for a crisis, here, a chastening artistic and personal failure. Communication between the two cinematic agents proceeds via the filmmaking process. With his obstructions, von Trier tries to show Leth what he thinks Leth is made of. With his obstruction films, Leth tries to demonstrate his mettle to von Trier. Fictions are produced in the course of this dialogue, as in #5: Avedøre where Leth must pretend to speak sincerely to von Trier. Or in the Brussels film where, perhaps, Leth imagines himself in the ideal image of the international Perfect Man of poetic mystery, played by Patrick Bauchau, who Leth admires for his 'well worn', life-experienced air. But these fictions are framed within a unifying nonfictional narrative. That narrative presents events in the communicative exchange between the co-authors. Were this narrative fictional, it would be sufficient for the purposes of critical appreciation simply to imagine them as happening – to imagine that von Trier assigns rules to Leth in order to trip him, that Leth interprets these rules in a series of embedded cinematic works, that von Trier eventually falls on his face because he has obstructed himself with a chastisement fantasy. However, on the evidence contained in the movie, it is more accurate to say that, rather than acting as if to do these things, von Trier and Leth really did them; and that they would have us believe this to be the case, and have us assert that these events occurred as part of the making of The Five Obstructions.

In Brussels, Leth aptly characterises his exchange with von Trier as a tennis match in which his opponent 'serves hard and we return hard as nails'. Granted, The Five Obstructions is not pure play. But what is? The idea of pure play is tough to defend. Arguably, play and the forms it takes exist partly because of adaptive, developmental ends they favour (see Bruner 1972; Bekoff & Byers 1998; Bateson 1999; Sutton-Smith 2001). Furthermore, play as such comports with extraneous interests. An activity, to count as play, needs to be inherently valuable for a given individual. From the person's own perspective it has the power to afford an intrinsically valued, engrossing experience of competition, chance, make-believe, vertigo, or some combination of these. An activity is play if and to just the degree that realising this intrinsic value is what matters most. The participant might also intend or desire the activity to serve other subjectively important utilities, though.

Play's psychological basis can change over time, especially when play is protracted or is that of the professionalised devotee of a game. The balance of motivation sustaining continued involvement might fluctuate. Playfulness can be eroded as play becomes mostly a means to other ends or economic imperatives become more onerous. Or it might become so encrusted with performative concerns that the participant retains only a vestigial sense of the activity's inherent pleasure. It is unlikely von Trier and Leth never suffered the *paidia*-killing tedium of filmmaking's practico-inert. Nor is it likely they had identical motives for the 5-O project. Leth, for instance, strikes me as simply humouring his nemesis's 'Help Jørgen Leth' scheme. Shared is an expectation that asymmetrical, agonistic interactions governed by ad hoc rules will yield a novel, stimulating experience of their cinematic work by infusing it, to different degrees for each participant, with pleasures of competition, chance, imagination and (inflicting) moral *ilinx*. Both also expect competition to stimulate and display their wits, echoing Caillois that struggle for dominance encourages players to focus and push their skills rather than rely on luck (1961: 15). As Leth, concluding his tennis metaphor, says: 'we have to pull our best shot out of the bag' to return von Trier's 'deadly' server. Psychologically framing their project as an agonistic, high-stakes game in which Leth risks his professional reputation and von Trier his implicit claim to equal if not greater mastery of cinematic agency transforms the work. It turns it into an escapade, makes the process less routine and boring while heightening its difficulty and emotional pitch.

To play is sometimes to accomplish great things: feats of athleticism or grace, cunning, technical virtuosity, delightful mimicry, engrossing fantasy, ingenious puzzle-solving, linguistic prowess. The prospect of pulling such shots out of the bag is a compelling reason to play because they are objects of inherent value; winning moves or not, they are ultimately desirable ends. They owe this inherent value to their potential to impart a feeling of satisfaction to the agent of their achievement, and potential to engage the attention of, and to incite pleasure in, the beholder. Instead of antithetical, as Caillois believes, play and art-making are conducive towards the same final ends: absorbing, intrinsically valued experiences and inherently valued achievements, for participants and observers alike. *The Five Obstructions* illuminates how work can be play within the sphere of art. True, von Trier proclaims his wish to provoke something of disvalue. But it is hard to believe he wanted or expected the film overall to be an artistic failure. The art work's premise – two expert cinematic practitioners trying to best one another – precludes that sort of nihilism and presupposes a competitive game worth playing that is also a spectacle worth watching.

WORKS CITED

Bateson, Gregory (1999) 'A Theory of Play and Fantasy', in Gregory Bateson, *Steps to an Ecology of Mind*. Chicago: University of Chicago Press, 177–93.

Bekoff, Marc and John Byers (eds) (1998) *Animal Play: Evolutionary, Comparative and Ecological Approaches*. Cambridge: Cambridge University Press.

Bratman, Michael (1992) 'Shared Cooperative Activity', *The Philosophical Review*, 101, 2, 327–41.

Bruner, Jerome (1972) 'The Nature and Uses of Immaturity', *American Psychologist*, 27, 8, 686–708.

Caillois, Roger (1961) *Man, Play, and Games*, trans. Meyer Barash. New York: Free Press.

Cameron, Ian and Mark Shivas (1963) 'Cinema A-Trite: A Survey Including Interviews with Richard Leacock, Albert and David Maysles, William Klein, Jean Rouch, and Jacques Rozier', *Movie*, 8, 22, 12–27.

Danish Film Institute (2002) *Film: Special Issue / Leth.* Copenhagen: Danish Film Institute.

Frankfurt, Harry (1989) 'Identification and Externality', in Harry Frankfurt, *The Importance of What We Care About.* Cambridge: Cambridge University Press, 58–68.

Gaut, Berys (1997) 'Film Authorship and Collaboration', in Richard Allen and Murray Smith (eds) *Film Theory and Philosophy.* Oxford: Oxford University Press, 149–72.

Levin, G. Roy (1971) *Documentary Explorations: 15 Interviews with Film-Makers.* New York: Doubleday.

Lewis, C. I. (1946) *An Analysis of Knowledge and Valuation.* La Salle, IL: Open Court.

Livingston, Paisley (1997) 'Cinematic Authorship', in Richard Allen and Murray Smith (eds) *Film Theory and Philosophy.* Oxford: Oxford University Press, 132–48.

____ (2004) 'C. I. Lewis and the Outlines of Aesthetic Experience', *British Journal of Aesthetics,* 44, 4, 378–92.

Morin, Edgar (2003) 'Chronicle of a Film', in Steven Feld (ed.) *Ciné-Ethnography: Jean Rouch.* Minneapolis: University of Minnesota Press, 229–65.

Plantinga, Carl (2005) 'What a Documentary Is, After All', *The Journal of Aesthetics and Art Criticism,* 63, 2, 105–17.

Ponech, Trevor (1999) *What Is Non-Fiction Cinema?: On the Very Idea of Motion Picture Communication.* Boulder, CO: Westview Press.

Rouch, Jean (2003) 'Ciné-Anthropolgy: Interview with Enrico Fulchignoni', in Steven Feld (ed.) *Ciné-Ethnography: Jean Rouch.* Minneapolis: University of Minnesota Press, 147–87.

Schepelern, Peter (2003) '"Kill Your Darlings": Lars von Trier and the Origins of Dogma 95', in Mette Hjort and Scott MacKenzie (eds) *Purity and Provocation: Dogma 95.* London: British Film Institute, 58–69.

Stecker, Robert (1997) *Artworks: Meaning, Definition, Value.* Stecker University Park: Pennsylvania State University Press.

Sutton-Smith, Brian (2001) *The Ambiguity of Play.* Cambridge, MA: Harvard University Press.

Von Trier, Lars and Thomas Vinterberg (2003 [1995]) 'The Vow of Chastity', in Mette Hjort and Scott MacKenzie (eds) *Purity and Provocation: Dogma 95.* London: British Film Institute, 199–200.

Wittgenstein, Ludwig (1968) *Philosophical Investigations,* trans. G. E. M. Anscombe. New York: Macmillan.

To Calculate the Moment: Leth's Life as Art

PETER SCHEPELERN

Jørgen Leth is generally considered to be one of the stars of contemporary Danish culture. He is a much admired and multi-talented figure, who has expressed himself in various media and always in ways that are clearly marked by a distinctive personality. He has managed to excel as a significant and eccentric artist who is unconstrained by commercial considerations, as a discriminating poet and filmmaker esteemed by the cultural elite. Leth has also managed to achieve a certain cult status in the eyes of the general public on account of his role as TV sports commentator for the Tour de France. Leth first assumed this role in 1989 and soon became known for his artistic diction and slightly nasal and sonorous voice. He has published poetry since 1962, and 2002 saw the publication of a collected edition of his nine books of poetry. Leth released his first film in 1963, and his cinematic oeuvre now includes more than forty titles, some of them shorts, others feature-length films. These works are all avant-garde films, and many are experimental documentaries, mostly about particular sports, artists and places. All are highly stylised and carefully crafted aesthetic products. Many of these films have enjoyed visibility on the festival circuit and at film museums, but the general public has been only dimly aware of them, if at all. *The Five Obstructions* became the occasion for Leth's late breakthrough in a broader context, also internationally. Finally, Leth is known for his attachment to Haiti, where he has lived on a permanent basis since 1991. His status as an expatriate has helped to brand him as a worldly cosmopolitan with attachments and interests far from the parish well.

Leth's artistic persona brings together key features of the contemporary Danish cultural world. He is a highly individualistic and controversial artist who insists on exploring new terrain, but he also willingly works within, and accepts the support of, a state-funded system. In some ways Leth has always been a rebel without a cause. His films and books have had no commercial potential, but this is exactly why he has been so appreciated as an uncompromising auteur. Leth's list of awards and honours is long, and in 1995 he was granted the Danish state's special support for outstanding artists, a lifelong pension. In 2000, the Danish Foreign Office appointed him honorary consul in Haiti.

Ever able to persuade the administrators of various public foundations and organisations to support his projects, Leth has been able to live the life of an eccentric artist, supplementing his artistic activities through work as a journalist, travel writer, jazz critic and sports commentator. What is more, Leth has always managed to frame this supplementary work in such a way that it became continuous somehow with his artistic endeavours. His general project, it seems, is a fusion of life and work, a wholly aestheticised approach to both life and art. What is important is not a given accomplishment, but the films, poetry and journalism as an integrated whole that expresses the life choices of a charismatic traveller and adventurer. Leth's life and art are designed to constitute a seductive *Gesamtkunstwerk*.

As a filmmaker, Leth appears as a kind of curator of a cinematographic museum filled with significant fragments. Here we find bits of reality, small chunks of time, all collected by a consummately artistic persona who gazes with unfailing fascination at a world for which he deftly manages to take no responsibility as a result of a strategy of supreme aestheticism. Leth looks at his own life with this very same mixture of distanced observation and phenomenological fascination, consistently blurring the boundary between life and work. In both life and art, his aim is to identify, seize and create significant moments – a kind of kairotic temporality – and the method underwriting this process involves seeing the world in a way that makes it 'strange'. Leth's preferred stance is that of the puzzled and fascinated, but also mock-scientific, observer. He enjoys adopting the role of the anthropologist whose distanced outsider's gaze is directed at a world that actually is strange and far away, and some of his films have taken him far from Denmark, to the US, to China, New Guinea and Haiti. At the same time, Leth also makes a point of casting a distanced look at worlds that are ordinary and wholly familiar. In *Life in Denmark* (*Livet i Danmark*, 1971), for example, which is one of his early master-pieces, Leth approaches his documentary task the way an anthropologist visiting a bizarre new world might. The same is true of *Aarhus* (2005), a film about Leth's childhood town. And in the now famous *The Perfect Human* (1967) he presents man and woman as extraordinary phenomena from another planet.

Major film essays like *Good and Evil* (*Det gode og det onde*, 1975) and *Notes on Love* (*Notater om kærligheden*, 1989) are kaleidoscopic and bizarre encyclopaedic reflections on various topics. *66 Scenes from America* (*66 scener fra Amerika*, 1982) and the sequel, *New Scenes from America* (*Nye scener fra Amerika*, 2002), are typical in this respect, for both films examine the United States in a number of tableaux, each scene speaking very much for itself. A quintessential Leth moment, one of the absolute best in his work, is the scene in *66 Scenes from America* where Andy Warhol is shown eating a hamburger in one uninterrupted 5-minute take. The scene takes place in (excruciating) silence until Warhol finally states: 'Ah ... My name is Andy Warhol and I just finished eating a hamburger.' Sitting there with his white wig, with the ketchup bottle and the crumpled paper from the hamburger, Warhol directs his slightly somnambulistic gaze towards the spectator and utters the line on which he and Leth had agreed. In this scene time, life and art fuse together in an empty sign in what is a quintes-sentially Warhol but also typically Leth moment.

Generally speaking, Leth has avoided anything resembling an epic flow or continuous narrative in his work. He has never written a novel, for while the book entitled *Traberg* is identified as a novel it is not in fact one. Similarly, the film called *Traberg* (1992) is not a fiction film but a kind of manipulated feature-length documentary about the political events that occurred in Haiti during the coup in 1991, all thinly disguised as fiction. Leth's one feature-length fiction film, *Haiti Express* (*Udenrigs-korrespondenten*, 1983), has no real plot, consisting only of fragmented scenes. The only films to make use of a kind of epic flow are the bicycle films, *The Stars and the Water Carriers* (*Stjernerne og vandbærerne*, 1974) and *A Sunday in Hell* (*En forårsdag i helvede*, 1976). Even here, though, it is the magical moment that counts, and the same can be said of Leth's poetry and TV commentaries. Leth describes the relevant technique in the following citation from *The Five Obstructions*:

> I normally find places and then isolate something I want to examine. That's the method. And then I frame it very precisely and wait for the right moment. I believe very strongly in waiting and observing.

The Five Obstructions is the triumphant result of Leth's aesthetical method, and it was probably the success of this film that made a book of memoirs seem like an obvious project. The book *The Imperfect Human* (*Det uperfekte menneske*), the title of which playfully refers to *The Five Obstructions*, presents the artist himself, his life in and through art, as perhaps the most challenging work of all. When the book came out, it created a media storm around the almost sacrosanct *flâneur* who insists on aestheticising his life. Leth's scandalous text is in many ways part of the effective history of his collaborative film, for it exposes the filmmaker's weaknesses in ways that von Trier's obstructions ultimately could not, highlighting, among other things, an unfortunate response to success.

Don't think you're special

Denmark has a perhaps somewhat undeserved reputation as an especially liberal and open society. The influential critic Georg Brandes (1842–1927) is a key figure in this liberal Danish tradition and also played an important role within the broader context of European modernity as an advocate for social and cultural innovation and freedom. The architect, poet, filmmaker and public intellectual Poul Henningsen (1894–1967) is also relevant here, for he is at the very centre of what is known as 'Danish cultural radicalism', a crucial leftwing trend that emerged in the inter-war period. *Kulturradikalismen* contributed values such as modernity, democracy, social consciousness and internationality to social and cultural debates in Denmark in the 1930s and continues to serve as a significant reference point within the landscape of contemporary debate. Yet Danish life is also characterised by other, far less open-minded traditions and in this connection the insights of the Danish-Norwegian writer Aksel Sandemose (1899–1965) are important. Sandemose saw society as implicitly governed by what he called the Law of Jante, and he used this fictional law to satirise the provincialism and self-righteousness of the most fundamental of Danish attitudes: *Don't think you're special or in any way more important than anyone else.*

In more recent times, the abolition of laws against pornography in 1967–69 and of film censorship for adult audiences was seen as a decisive victory for cultural radicalism over darker reactionary forces. In the late 1960s freedom from state control and censorship was celebrated in the name of free speech and human liberty. Danes momentarily had free access to what some liberal proponents of freedom of expression considered the bliss of pornography. Yet it soon became apparent that pornography signalled only freedom for a male audience and relied on the oppression of women.

More recently, Denmark has witnessed a number of cultural controversies that have generated considerable attention, both nationally and internationally, and these controversies have both challenged and brought into focus the limits of Danish openness. As is well known, 12 satirical drawings depicting Mohammed and commissioned by the newspaper *Jyllands-Posten* in September 2005 had the effect of producing a 'cartoon crisis' that created a kind of global interest in Denmark that most Danes would rather have done without. In the summer of 2003 the Danish vicar Thorkild Grosbøll announced that he did not believe in 'a creative and sustaining God', and the story of the vicar who did not believe in God also reverberated abroad. And then there was the Jørgen Leth scandal that erupted in response to the publication (on 29 September 2005) of his memoirs.

The Imperfect Human contains two controversial elements – Leth's ultimately less interesting revelations about his activities as a hash smuggler in the 1970s, and his confessions about his sexual relations with young Haitian women. The Leth controversy focused on the latter revelations, and particularly on one chapter in which the author describes his relationship, as a man over sixty, with a 17-year-old girl who is his cook's daughter. Two sentences from this chapter were cited over and again in the media: 'I take the cook's daughter whenever I want to. It is my right' (2005: 308).

The book was reviewed by seven Danish newspapers when it first came out. The reviewers, all men, generally praised its style and entertainment value; the sexual theme was mentioned, but in an ironic rather than condemning manner. The Copenhagen tabloid *Ekstra Bladet* published an appreciative critique by their usual reviewer, an academic critic, who was 'enormously impressed by the original form' and ended by saying that 'you swallow it scene by scene and would wish that it went on and on' (Jørgensen 2005). The editorial office took a rather different line, however, sparking what would become a media furore with front-page headlines such as 'Leth held 17 year old as Sex Slave' (*Ekstra Bladet*, 29 September 2005, cited in Johnsen 2005: 12). *Ekstra Bladet* earns a considerable portion of its income from sex advertisements and has traditionally stood for a certain popular frankness about sex and nudity; in addition this tabloid has made a point over the years of publishing gleefully vicious attacks on celebrities, and especially artists with modernist inclinations, the implicit assumption apparently being that most Danes are inclined to see such artists as arrogant parasites on the welfare state's overly generous host body. The journalist who conducted the interview with Leth on the occasion of his book's publication actually resigned in anger from *Ekstra Bladet* when it became clear to him that his material had been seriously distorted by the tabloid's editors. Explaining his resignation, this journalist indicated that the distortions had made him the 'involuntary executioner' of a man he respected (Moe 2005).

While *Ekstra Bladet*'s motivations for attacking Leth were transparently self-serving, other dailies with a less crass and pragmatic profile echoed the basic charges. *Politiken*, for example, the main exponent of cultural radicalism, published an editorial identifying the filmmaker as a 'lecher' (6 October 2005, cited in Johnsen 2005: 20). Other interventions brought outraged citizens, and especially feminists, into the fray, and many viewed Leth as an unscrupulous hedonist, as a dirty old man involved in abusing poor young women from a third world country. In October alone, Danish newspapers published more than 500 letters, articles and editorials about Leth and his memoirs; the case was also exposed in the Haitian press (*Haiti News Brief*, 5 and 11 October 2005).

Overwhelmed by the virulence of the attacks, Leth chose to remain silent and went underground. Initiatives were, however, undertaken to defend him. A supportive homepage, for example, gathered three thousand signatures, and Lars von Trier and a number of colleagues – mostly younger directors such as Thomas Vinterberg, Lone Scherfig, Ole Christian Madsen, Per Fly, Annette K. Olesen and Tómas Gislason – published a statement in which they registered their support for Leth in the face of what they called 'a neo-puritanical witch hunt directed at one of the country's most prominent artists' (von Trier *et al.* 2005).

The debate culminated after two weeks when Leth chose to resign as honorary consul. The Foreign Office's response made it clear that Leth was right to assume that he could no longer be 'Our Man in Haiti'. Within this same period, TV2 terminated Leth's contract as sports commentator, thereby bringing a fruitful 18-year-long partnership to an end. TV2 made an announcement to the effect that the station respected Leth's artistic freedom but also had to defend its own values. When the Leth controversy erupted, the Danish Film Institute had already committed preliminary financial support to the filmmaker's projected documentary entitled *The Erotic Human* (*Det erotiske menneske*). This film, it became known, was to include a scene in which a young Haitian woman has intercourse with Leth. For some time, the Institute withstood the pressure of the media furore and tried to defend Leth. Henning Camre, CEO of the Danish Film Institute, is a close friend of Leth's, having worked as his cinematographer on *Notes on Love*. Eventually, however, the Institute also found it necessary to distance itself from Leth, in this instance through a withdrawal of the allocated monies for *The Erotic Human*.

Let them blush at my depravity

Leth's book is not a chronological tale or conventional biography. The memoirs are consistent with his usual artistic practice, the point being to use short pieces of prose to explore a number of impressionistic scenes. The subtitle draws attention to Leth's preferred approach: '*Scenes from my Life*'. In many ways the book presents a 'Life Chopped into Pieces', as one section is tellingly entitled (2005: 130).

Genre-wise, the book belongs to a long tradition of candid memoirs. Jean-Jacques Rousseau, of course, is the central figure in this field, and Leth seems implicitly to agree with the view that the author of *The Confessions* (1782) famously articulated in its introduction: 'Let them listen to my confessions, let them blush at my depravity, let them tremble at my sufferings; let each in his turn expose with equal sincerity the failings, the wanderings of his heart, and if he dare, aver, I was better than that man.' Sexuality and erotic conquests are thematised at length in Leth's text, and his pointed frankness about these matters bring Casanova, Frank Harris and Henry Miller into play as obvious implicit references.

The reader of Leth's memoirs learns about the passion that he experiences when his second wife experiments with the role of call girl (2005: 154) and when a friend later arranges to sleep with his third wife (2005: 266). The key point is that the book describes a large number of sexual encounters, often with young women in exotic settings. For the most part, these encounters are intensely sensuous and physical, rather than deeply personal, experiences. A typical story is the one in which Leth figures as a reporter in Africa in 1962. He remembers being taken to a tribal feast, and a girl being chosen for his pleasure: 'She was mine for that night. She was shy. I could not speak to her. We did not understand each other's words. She quickly undressed' (2005: 86). Leth similarly recalls how he met a French woman as a young man on a Nile cruise, and how he ended up moving from his own economy-class cabin to her first-class cabin: 'I must conclude that I have a talent for being upgraded. For there is no reason to call it a talent for hustling' (2005: 80). There are also stories about a young German woman in Egypt (2005: 78), South-Americans (2005: 121), the Jewish Rachelle (2005: 141), girls in Rio (2005: 256), a young Israeli woman (2005: 278) – and the Haitian girls, Yvrodie (2005: 297), Dorothie (the daughter of Leth's cook) (2005: 308, 322) and Rose-anna (2005: 338). 'The elderly man excited by the young woman. Again, again', Leth says (2005: 339).

Here we meet the frank raconteur, the seducer bragging about his conquests, but also a man stating facts, coming clean: this is what happened, this is what I did. The analytical aesthete seems to be standing at the bedside watching the activities of his double, his alter ego, as a kind of self-voyeurism:

> I am obsessed by this young body that stretches and arches and opens itself for me on the white sheet. Is it the fantasy of possession that makes me so wild? Is it what is forbidden? Is it the erotic vision of colonialism that comes seeping from the back of my head, creating a double exposure of this scene so that I am both in the middle of it and can watch it from the outside? This young native girl, who becomes a woman and sighs and surrenders under me. Her approachability intoxicates me. My own age is part of the staggering contract. (2005: 310)

Leth also provides a description of how the love scene with Dorothie – the one originally to have been included in his next documentary – was shot. The cinematographer framed only Dorothie's face, while Leth had sex with her from behind:

> It didn't take many seconds before intercourse was really happening, and I have to admit that the whole arrangement was terribly exciting, also for her, I believe … Afterwards I was very happy, very proud. I thought that I had now produced something that had never been produced by any other director. I thought that I had crossed a boundary in the art of documentary filmmaking. I thought of self-sacrifice and fire. I thought that I was much further out here than even Godard had been. (2005: 322)

It is interesting to note that Leth imagines himself as the only director in the world to have produced such images. He sees himself as somehow being up against an art-film guru like Godard, whom he (like most art-film people who started in the 1960s) has always admired; but he should in fact be looking somewhere else entirely for parallels. Experimental film has, of course, often focused on sex. Examples include Stan Brakhage's *Loving* (1957) and Andy Warhol's *Blue Movie* (1969); and Carolee Schneemann actually had her own lovemaking filmed in *Fuses* (1967). But, if we look beyond the small world of avant-garde film, we quickly notice that the theme of the director's sexual involvement has in fact been quite thoroughly explored. Indeed, there is actually an entire category of modern porn flicks that share the very feature that Leth finds so novel. Pornographers like Ed Powers and others have produced thousands of scenes of the kind that Leth describes. Their films belong to the so-called 'Pro-Am' genre, which typically involves an older male director having sex with a young woman, and in some cases even filming the process himself.

It is perhaps in his understanding of the relation of life to art that Leth appears as an essentially, or wilfully, naïve traveller. He frequents the artistic, aesthetic world as a splendid but remote and somehow parallel universe. He sees the sexual experiments with his wives as an exciting way of exploring life; to others these experiences might simply register as expressions of a swinger culture or, more critically, as indications of a promiscuous attitude. When Leth has sex with impoverished young women, he views the encounter as an artistic act with sensuality as the motivating factor; others are likely to view this act as a purely exploitative arrangement that locks a poor woman into the powerful grip of a wealthy man. Whereas Leth feels that he is surpassing Godard and making groundbreaking art films, others may well be inclined to think that he has stepped into the far more straightforward world of pornography.

A key feature of Leth's art and life has to do, perhaps, with his inability to distinguish between the aesthetic universe of eccentric artistry and the banal universe of ordinary reality. This blurring of boundaries is what made Leth intensely controversial in the autumn of 2005, but it is also the very basis for his artistic creativity. Leth understands his artist's world as being governed by rules and values that are specific to it. Viewed from the perspective of ordinary reality, the actions performed in this world appear in a very different light, one that makes them seem only problematic. There can be no doubt that Leth was the victim of a media storm involving motives that were neither idealistic nor sincere. At the same time, Leth revealed himself to be remarkably unaware of certain basic realities. He was misunderstood because he naïvely took his artificial paradise to be a true picture of the world.

In Bergman's famous *The Seventh Seal* (*Det sjunde inseglet*, 1957), a medieval allegory, the mountebank tries to escape Death and pleads: 'Aren't there special rules for actors?' Generally, there *are* special rules for actors and other artists. There is a strong need, at least since the Romantic period, to see the artist as an almost separate species of being, capable of using talent to challenge conventionality. This need helps to explain the existence of a tradition of tolerance for the eccentricity of artists' lifestyles. It would in many ways be rather disappointing to learn that great artists are perfectly ordinary people with a garage and a pension scheme. Artists, after all, are not supposed to be concerned with material accoutrements and the kind of strategic safeguards against risk that are so typical of a middle-class life.

What the Leth case shows is that there are limits to the tolerance on which artists have traditionally been able to draw. Leth's originality as an artist is all about an ability to mobilise considerable artistic talent in order to reveal an aesthetically challenging, but also wholly seductive and hypnotic vision of the world. It was inevitable, in a sense, that reality would catch up with him sooner or later. And reality – with its media circuses, its political correctness and its Jante Law – has ground rules that are quite different from those governing experimental art. In the universe of art, obstructions can become a vehicle for new and surprising insights. If you use a similar strategy in the real world you just fall flat on your face.

Leth interprets his carnality, his 'self-sacrifice and fire' (perhaps a nod to Humbert Humbert who calls his nymphet 'fire of my loins' in Nabokov's *Lolita*) as a kind of connection to other artists. His controversial memoirs mention Graham Greene, whose novel *The Quiet American* (1955) has similar themes (2005: 346). In Greene's story a middle-aged British journalist in Indo-China helps to murder a young American, partly because the young man has been involved in cynical political machinations, partly because the victim is about to steal away his lovely young Vietnamese mistress. The 18-year-old Phuong is characterised as the personification of sexual compliance – 'She did at once what I asked … she would have made love if I had asked her to, straight away, peeling off her trousers without question' (Greene 1973: 127). Another passage repeats the point: 'She gently and sweetly laid out her body for my pleasure' (1973: 155). The narrator, who shares many features with the author, describes the nature of his motivations succinctly: 'I only want her body' (1973: 60; see also Sherry 1996: 409).

The Gauguin Syndrome

Leth's interest in Greene was also one of the reasons why the Danish filmmaker became interested in Haiti. Leth admired 'the nearly surrealist atmosphere of horror that is created' (2005: 237) in Greene's *The Comedians* (1966) and thus chose Haiti as the setting for his feature film about a foreign correspondent. Leth went to Haiti on a research trip in 1981 and shot most of *Haiti Express* there. He returned to Haiti in 1991, taking up permanent residence in Jacmel. Leth has involved himself in the local community, and has followed the chaotic situation in the country as a sympathetic observer. It is his world, but at the same time he sees himself as a guest. From an artistic point of view Haiti has been stimulating, just as the country has provided a refuge where Leth could recover from periods of mental depression. But there can be little doubt that sensuality also helps to explain Leth's interest in Haiti.

Leth's self-revelations in *The Imperfect Human* were presented as sensational and new in the autumn of 2005, but there was in fact nothing particularly novel about his confessions. Leth has been variously involved in thematising his relations with young Haitian women for more than a decade. In this sense his memoirs are but the culmination of a long process of voluntary self-exposure, as if he, again and again, has been asking to be found out – and to be forgiven.

In *Haiti Express* there is a scene where the restless, melancholic white European visits a black prostitute. But apart from that, it is still the European woman, played by Hanne Uldal (Leth's wife at the time), who is the focus of the white man's desire. In a characteristic scene we see the woman lying naked on the bed while the dialogue unfolds as follows:

Woman: I want to be used by you.

Man: You have a wet cunt.

Woman: I am yours. You can use me as you wish.

This fantasy about female submission has long been an anachronistic male fantasy in Western culture (where, it could be argued, it constitutes the basis for pornography) but it may still be connected to deeply rooted traditions in other cultures. *Notes on Love*, one of Leth's most personal films, is a fragmented collection of staged incidents – ballet dancers dancing, a man who has problems taking his jacket off, Leth shaving, a man (Leth) and a woman lying naked on a bed – and documentary shots. The documentary footage consists primarily of material resulting from a journey to the Trobriand Islands, where Leth and his crew saw themselves as following in the footsteps of the famous anthropologist Bronislaw Malinowski. The latter carried out crucial research in this part of the world during World War One and the film clearly expresses Leth's admiration for his achievements: 'Malinowski is my hero', the voice-over states. Leth is fascinated by Malinowski's attitude, by the very idea of the scientific researcher who casts his distanced gaze at the most intimate of subject matters in the manner of a kind of ingenious but disinterested and properly anthropological Sherlock Holmes. The film shows photos of Malinowski (wearing a white pith helmet) together with naked indigenous people from Melanesia. These photos are intercut with Leth's footage from the same place. Leth's approach is to combine reconstructions of Malinowski's photos with entirely new shots by Leth and with shots showing Leth and Camre shooting their film. The film contrasts Western civilisation with the other world. We see the half-naked indigenous women, both the footage itself and the process of shooting it. A recurrent motif in the film shows the stem of a boat gliding down a river in the tropical twilight, accompanied by Schubert's String Quintet and hints at a sexual symbolism of penetration.

Malinowski claims that his description of the sexual mores of the Trobrianders cannot 'be of any use to the seeker after pornography' (2001: xxiii), but clearly these customs have artistic potential as far as Leth is concerned. His interest focuses on Malinowski's *The Sexual Life of Savages* from 1929, and on this book only,[1] which confirms that what is at issue here is artistic inspiration rather than scientific curiosity. Playfully and ironically, Leth uses Malinowski's attitude as a general aesthetic method. Malinowski's serious scientific project is replaced by an experiment with life and art. And Leth, unlike Malinowski, is willing to participate directly in the sexual life of the savages, thereby crossing the line that separates participation from observation. Some years later Leth would clearly identify this characteristic investment in the blurring and transgression of boundaries:

> I am an absolute champion when it comes to living and at the same time observing myself. It is my cross to bear, in a way, but that's the way it is. It is also my profession. I will always be able to observe myself and to see myself as an image ... This is precisely the origin of art. (Quoted in Johnsen 2005: 127)

Tómas Gislason, who was initially known primarily as one of Lars von Trier's early collaborators, made his directorial debut with a documentary portrait of Leth entitled *Heart and Soul* (*Fra hjertet til hånden*, 1994). Here Leth talks about his relationship with his Haitian lover Yvrodie, who is also in the film. Leth describes how he once heard somebody who had seen them together exclaim: 'Look at the little slave sitting there cutting the toe nails of the white man!' And he goes on to add: 'In the very moment this threshold is crossed, you experience yourself in precisely that light.' Leth seems to be surprised that a relationship that he himself sees as a relationship between consenting adults can be interpreted in terms of master/slave dynamics, but in the memoirs he himself draws attention to 'the erotic vision of colonialism' that keeps returning (2005: 310).

In 1994 Leth made a contribution to a book called *Brøndums Encyklopædi*, a title humorously referencing the 20-volume *Great Danish Encyclopaedia* that began to appear the same year. Leth's article was entitled 'Cunt' and it explains the Haitian woman's pragmatic attitude to sex and the body, as he understands it:

> In Haiti the woman in the countryside sees the cunt as an estate, a piece

of land that she owns. She talks about it as 'my little plot of land'. What she
has between her legs is what she has to do business with and trade with.
The cunt is her commodity. By trading reasonably she can achieve a position in life. She knows what she can give. She has her little plot of land
and it is an asset that she will invest sensibly. (Bentzen *et al.* 1994: 170)

Leth's ambitious documentary, *Haiti. Untitled* (*Haiti. Uden titel*) premiered
in 1996. This film describes a country of poverty, political violence and
chaos, murders and voodoo, all shown without an explanatory voice-over.
In one scene we see half-naked young Haitian women washing – and
washing themselves – in the river. We see the poet Sophie Déstin (wrongly identifed in the credits as Sophie Désir!), who reclines naked in a chair
while she recites her poem 'Je suis une femme'. After a long sequence involving violence, the military and politics, the film ends with four shots of
a naked young woman smiling at the camera from a bed. In an interview
book, Leth identifies the woman as 'my then girlfriend Yvrodie who in a
very graceful scene lies naked on a bed' (quoted in Leifer 1999: 221), and
then continues to proffer the following analysis:

> It is rather personal material that circles around what I call the Gauguin
> Syndrome: A white man who gets fascinated by a black woman ... My
> reasoning was that I could not make this film as an honest testimony
> about the fascinations of Haiti without including this woman ... What
> speaks to me most strongly in Haiti is the sensuality. (1999: 227)

Paul Gauguin, who also left a Danish marriage to find fulfilment and artistic inspiration through relationships with very young indigenous women
elsewhere, used a similar motif in some of his most famous paintings, including *Spirit of the Dead Watching* (1892, Albright-Knox Art Gallery, Buffalo)
and *Nevermore* (1897, Courtauld Institute, London), both of which depict
a naked Tahitian girl on a bed (see also Danielsson 1965).

In a long newspaper interview from 2001, 'The White Man' (reprinted
in Johnsen), Leth elaborates on the Gauguin Syndrome:

> The essence of love is an ongoing negotiation and I feel that I spend a lot

of time negotiating the conditions that allow love to be carried out and eroticism to unfold … I call it the Gauguin Syndrome. The fact of being in a country and falling in love with the country and its women. I want to be the white man with the black woman. My desire is precisely for the deeply rooted power position in relation to that woman. For me it is a clear urge. I can feel that for me it is becoming more and more impossible with intellectual, white women. They don't attract me any longer. (Johnsen 2005: 115–16)

At play here is a middle-aged man who prefers young women to those of his own age, a phenomenon known from most cultures; but here combined with a kind of cultural disgust for 'intellectual, white women'.

It doesn't matter

Two weeks after the storm erupted, Leth answered his critics in an interview, 'Forhør' ('Interrogation'; reprinted in Johnsen 2005). In his defence, Leth insisted that he is no Casanova who hunts women; at no point, he claimed, did he 'use power' (Johnsen 2005: 120). As for the sentence that had become the infamous spark for moral outrage – having the 'right' to take the cook's daughter – Leth's explanation was as follows:

It's a game I play … For it is clear that sexuality involves a lot of power and many games. And many of these games take place in my head. I play the power game in my own head. (Johnsen 2005: 121)

In a recent work by Philip Roth, the grand old man of frank sexuality in modern American prose, a similar case is presented. In the short novel *The Dying Animal* (2001), a 62-year-old university professor has an affair with a 24-year-old Cuban woman called Consuela, who is his voluptuous student. In the 'White Man' interview Leth makes the following statements:

It is intoxicating to be the white man. It is intoxicating to possess the power. I have felt that the black woman's interest for the white man is something instinctive. It has its roots in some very deep social, historical reasons, the whole history of Haiti, slavery, I am not blind to that, but I feel that the interest is primarily erotic. (Johnsen 2005: 116)

In Roth's novel the narrator explains:

There is no sexual equality and there can be no sexual equality, certainly not one where the allotments are equal, the male quotient and the female quotient in perfect balance. There's no way to negotiate metrically this wild thing. It's not fifty-fifty like a business transaction. It's the chaos of eros we're talking about, the radical destabilisation that is its excitement. (2001: 20).

In his book Leth comments on the age question: 'My own age is part of the staggering contract' (2005: 310), and in the interview in which he defends his actions he asks:

But isn't there a kind of age fascism here? How long is a man allowed to be sexually active? ... The outcry is less about the age of the girl than it is about my age. But who should be allowed to decide the issue? (Johnsen 2005: 125)

In Roth's novel a similar line of defence is adopted:

Now, most people are appalled by the vast difference in age, but it is the very thing Consuela is drawn to. The erotic oddness is all that people register, and they register it as repugnance, as repugnant farce. But the age I am has great significance for Consuela. These girls with old gents don't do it despite the age – they're drawn to the age, they do it *for* the age. Why? In Consuela's case, because the vast difference in age gives her permission to submit, I think. My age and my status give her, rationally, the license to surrender, and surrendering in bed is a not unpleasant sensation. But simultaneously, to give yourself over intimately to a much, much older man provides this sort of younger woman with authority of a kind she cannot get in a sexual arrangement with a younger man. She gets both the pleasures of submission *and* the pleasures of mastery. (2001: 32)

Leth talks about how *he*, not she, was seduced. Coming of age in Haiti means being streetwise and sophisticated, he claims. The key question, however, is whether Leth's sexual exploits involve instrumental attitudes.

> Absolutely, it is always like that in Haiti. That's life in Haiti. Everybody wants something from everybody … It is a common way of thinking in Haiti and it holds for all things in life. And it also holds for sex, of course. (Johnsen 2005: 122)

The journalist Poul Pilgaard Johnsen eventually contacted Dorothie Laguerre, the young woman who was filmed in connection with *The Erotic Human*. She defended Leth and had nothing but praise for him, thereby apparently supporting his contention that exploitation was not an element in the exchange (Johnsen 2005: 78ff).

In the spring of 2006 Leth published a new volume of poetry, *It doesn't matter (Det gør ikke noget)*, reflecting the affair. In several poems there is 'a black woman on a white sheet' (2006: 53), mainly in the long 'The photographer is possibly desirous' ('Fotografen har muligvis lyst', 59ff). 'The Danish language' ('Det danske sprog') is about the shooting of *The Erotic Human* and in this poem Leth evokes 'the anthropologist who fucks his woman' (2006: 124). The poet also admits that he is 'Guilty of fucking young women', but claims to 'have loved them all' (2006: 125).

Most media storms typically follow the same pattern: they escalate quickly and after the culmination they subside just as quickly. Early in 2006, the weekly newspaper *Weekendavisen* awarded Leth a prestigious literary award based on a readers' poll. In May 2006 the Danish Film Institute announced that it had decided, after all, to support the production of *The Erotic Human* (although with certain provisos). And in July, Leth was greeted with enormous enthusiasm by fans at a reading at the Rock Festival in Roskilde. In 2007 Leth published the second volume of his memoirs, *The Gold at the Bottom of the Sea (Guldet på havets bund)*, where he comments on the case against him and also tells about new encounters with young women. Milder winds are blowing.

Leth with the black dancer in *#1: Cuba*

Sex obstructions

Lars von Trier, Leth's sparring partner and collaborator in *The Five Ob-structions*, has always circled around sexuality and perversion. The early amateur film, *Menthe la Bienheureuse* (1979), is an unofficial adaptation of Pauline Réage's *Histoire d'O* (1954). *Forbrydelsens element* (*The Element of Crime*, 1984) includes rather graphic sex scenes between the detective and the prostitute; *Breaking the Waves* (1996) was originally planned as a Mar-quis de Sade adaptation and focuses on sexual degradation; and *Dogville* (2003) pursues this theme further within the context of a revenge story. It is interesting to note, however, that there is nothing in von Trier's ob-structions that invites Leth into the erotic sphere. Leth's decision to bring erotic elements into play in the remakes appears to be entirely his own.

In *#1: Cuba* Leth is seen standing behind the young Cuban woman and in the next sequence she is naked. When Leth is instructed to make his own remake of *The Perfect Human*, without any explicit directions from von Trier (Obstruction #3), he chooses to develop a little erotic story about a middle-aged man in a hotel in Brussels. This man meets a seductive Belgian woman, but we also see him having sex with a black

woman and the narrative hints at travels to Caracas. In the cartoon sequence (*#4: Cartoon*) we see animated versions of scenes from *Good and
Evil* (the one in which a naked woman is shown reclining on a sofa), as
well as scenes from *Notes on Love*. The scenes from the latter film focus on
Leth with a female partner (both naked), and on a river boat, a recurring
motif in the original film.

Von Trier has always been drawn to self-flagellation and in recent times
he has made a point of trying to share his approach with other filmmakers. Dogma 95 proposed a kind of methodical programme of self-punish-
ment that filmmakers might pursue in the manner of a cure. Viewed in
this light, *The Five Obstructions* appears to be an attempt to find a special
punishment/cure that speaks directly to Leth's special needs. Leth's willingness to accept von Trier's game strongly suggests that he is ready to
undergo the proposed treatment, that he is ready, more precisely, to punish himself. In this connection the many examples of sexual confessions,
culminating with the memoirs, can be seen as a desire for punishment or
at least subjugation. The hedonist, it would seem, longs for transfiguration,
and artistic fulfilment, through obstructions and punishment.

Leth survived the ordeals that von Trier had designed for him in *The
Five Obstructions* virtually unscathed. Von Trier tried hard to challenge
Leth's innocence and to confront him with reality, perhaps as an attempt
to test life and art against each other. The only thing that happened as a
result was that *The Five Obstructions* became Leth's masterpiece. And when
Leth was brought down some two years later, the cause was not to be
sought in various subtle aesthetic challenges, but in some rather simple
mechanisms of ordinary reality. Public discourse made Leth's fall seem
momentous, but entirely overlooked the extent to which this filmmaker,
circling around his Gauguin Syndrome, has long sought some form of
punishment and humiliation.

Leth makes experimental films and he makes a point of living his life
as a kind of experiment. He is very aware that he is looking for a certain
aesthetic order and for some form of aesthetic fulfilment in life. Bicycling,
art, sex, these are all activities that can be made into scenes or tableaux,
that can be transformed into magical, frozen moments. Leth can be seen
as unwittingly connecting with one of the great Danish classics, for in

many ways his approach is that of Kierkegaard's aesthete:

> You are witty, ironic, observant, a dialectician, experienced in enjoyment. You know how to calculate the moment; you are sentimental, heartless, all according to the circumstances; but during all this you are at all times only in the moment, and for that reason your life disintegrates, and it is impossible for you to explain it. (1987: 179)

Impossible or not, *The Imperfect Human* is Jørgen Leth explaining his life of moments.

NOTE

1   See Leifer 1999: 146; in Hjort & Bondebjerg 2001: 63, Leth mistakenly identifies the book as *Sex and Repression in Savage Society*.

WORKS CITED

Bentzen, Peer, Niels Lyngsø, Iselin C. Hermann, Astrid Pejtersen, Morten Søndergaard (eds) (1994) *Brøndums Encyklopædi*. Copenhagen: Brøndum.

Danielsson, Bengt (1965) *Gauguin in the South Seas*. New York: Doubleday.

Greene, Graham (1973) *The Quiet American*, in *The Collected Edition*, vol. 11. London: Heinemann.

Haiti News Brief (2005) Available at: www.haitisupport.gn.apc.org (accessed 16 October 2005)

Hjort, Mette and Ib Bondebjerg (2001) *The Danish Directors. Dialogues on a Contemporary National Cinema*. Bristol: Intellect.

Johnsen, Poul Pilgaard (ed.) (2005) *Det fordømte menneske*. Copenhagen: People's Press.

Jørgensen, John Chr. (2005) 'Bog: Mageløst rå og artistisk', *Ekstra Bladet*, 29 September.

Kierkegaard, Søren (1987 [1843]) *Either/Or*, trans. and ed. Howard V. Hong and Edna H. Hong. Princeton: Princeton University Press.

Leifer, Anders (1999) *Også i dag oplevede jeg noget...* Copenhagen: Information.

Leth, Jørgen (2005) *Det uperfekte menneske*. Copenhagen: Gyldendal.

_____ (2006) *Det gør ikke noget*. Copenhagen: Gyldendal.

_____ (2007) *Guldet på havets bund. Det uperfekte menneske/2*. Copenhagen: Gyldendal.

Malinowski, Bronislaw (2001 [1929]) *The Sexual Life of Savages*. Honolulu: The University Press of the Pacific.

Moe, Jacob Berner (2005) 'Den ufrivillige bøddel', *Journalisten*, 17. Available at: http://journalisten.inforce.dk/sw6577.asp (accessed 20 March 2008).

Roth, Philip (2001) *The Dying Animal*. London: Vintage Books.

Rousseau, Jean-Jacques (1782) *The Confessions of J.J. Rousseau*. Available at: www.fullbooks.com (accessed 19 December 2006).

Sherry, Barry (1996) *The Life of Graham Greene*, vol. 2. New York: Penguin.

Von Trier, Lars *et al.* (2005) 'Press release', *Berlingske Tidende*, 8 October.

Funny Games

MURRAY SMITH

What's eating Lars von Trier ?

Throughout *The Five Obstructions*, Lars von Trier rails against what he terms the 'provocative, perverse perfection' that he believes Jørgen Leth, or at any rate his films, embody. Von Trier sets himself against this 'perfection', variously depicting himself as the scourge of corruption, the therapist seeking to cure his patient, and the iconoclast seeking to tear down a false god. But let's back up a bit and see if we can bring the conceptual target of von Trier's ire into sharper focus. Karen Hanson, in an essay on the relationship between moral and aesthetic value, provides a useful way into this matter:

> Worries about the immorality of art can arise from a number of apparently quite different considerations. One line of thought … is grounded on an assumption that art is removed, or removes us, from life and thus from the strictures and obligations that properly bind us. This anxiety may stand as a vexed tribute to the cultural power of the doctrine of art for art's sake. It may be that Oscar Wilde's claim that 'All art is quite useless' is granted, but the claim is treated as an anguished accusation and not a proud proclamation. (1998: 204)

Von Trier's vexation seems to go back a long way in his personal history – as far back, at least, as his encounter with the film that inspires *The Five Obstructions*, Jørgen Leth's 1967 short *The Perfect Human*. In the first scene of *The Five Obstructions*, von Trier refers to Leth's film as 'a little gem that we are now going to ruin'. The new film will be both the record and enactment of a contest in which von Trier will seek to shatter the perfection of *The Perfect Human*, while Leth attempts to preserve it.[1] What is it about this film that so draws von Trier's admiration and contempt? Exactly how does Leth's early short embody the 'perfection' that von Trier finds so troubling?

The Perfect Human is an enigmatic, spare narrative film, depicting a man and a woman engaged in various generic activities – eating, dancing, undressing, shaving – mostly in isolation from one another. Interwoven with these familiar actions are a number of cryptic statements and gestures ('today I saw something that I hope to understand…'), articulated by the male character or by the voice-over that provides a running commentary on what we see. The setting of the film is abstract in the extreme: the performers are afforded certain minimal props (a razor, a bed, a dining table) but the space behind them is so overexposed as to lead the eye into a white void. The man and the woman are beautiful, young, chic; much of the time they are doing little more than *striking poses* in the featureless zone that they occupy. The film thus evokes a range of divergent sources: symbolist and absurdist theatre, art cinema (such as that of Ingmar Bergman, and Alain Resnais' *Last Year in Marienbad* (*L'Année dernière à Marienbad*, 1961) in particular come to mind), but also fashion imagery. All of this makes sense when we think of the year – 1967 – in which *The Perfect*

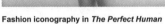
Fashion iconography in *The Perfect Human*

Human was released. But of course, this was also the year that Jean-Luc Godard, a filmmaker who had engaged with many of these same cultural currents, made *Weekend*, the film in which the formal and allusive playfulness of his earlier films becomes laced with a bitter awareness of contemporary political reality. Set alongside a film like *Weekend*, *The Perfect Human* looks like art film frippery. It is too detached, too inward-looking, too self-satisfied. It embodies a form of highbrow escapism. It is the product of an *aesthete's* sensibility, in just the sense captured by Hanson.

Is this a fair characterisation of *The Perfect Human?* Perhaps not entirely – the droll and ironic tone of the film, and the very explicitness with which it engages with the notion of 'perfection', suggest something other than a simple acceptance of the notion, or of any one model of perfection. Nevertheless, it is fair to say that this is the role that *The Perfect Human* plays in *The Five Obstructions*, at least as von Trier sees it. In the dialogue in which von Trier and Leth discuss in most depth their approach to filmmaking and their beliefs about art, von Trier continually emphasises the importance of error, lack of control and the unintentional: for example, the greatest gift an actor can give you, he claims, is to 'fuck up', thereby stumbling upon a possibility no one had foreseen. In short, von Trier extols the virtues of *imperfection*. Leth, in turn, assumes his role in this drama, accusing von Trier of extolling 'pure romanticism', and early on in the film cursing him for his purely 'destructive' obstructions.

The limitation to shots no longer than 12 frames – half a second – in the first obstruction is the immediate source of Leth's anger: 'It'll be a spastic film.' This constraint, challenging enough on its own terms, was probably chosen by von Trier precisely to target Leth's known preference for long takes.[2] Leth's resourcefulness in meeting this challenge, however – 'The 12 frames are a paper tiger!' he declares, relaxing in a Hockneyesque swimming pool of luminous blue – will drive von Trier to adopt much more direct assaults on the ideal of perfection that he attributes to Leth. The second obstruction is surely the bluntest attack of all. For this version von Trier decrees that the film must be shot in the worst place on earth that Leth can think of, and that Leth must play the role of the protagonist of *The Perfect Human.* The reality of Leth's ageing body is thus set against Claus Nissen's perpetually youthful, Dorian Gray-like hero, his stylish appearance preserved in the 'aspic' of film. During *#2: Bombay*, our memory of Leth's victorious swim is likely to be displaced by an earlier moment, immediately following his complaint about the 12-frame limitation. Bleary-eyed in bed as dawn rises in Havana, Leth's age weighs heavily upon him as he moans: 'This is too much. It's too difficult.'

The game of style

Serious issues are at stake, then, but the dialogue around them is to be conducted in the form of a game. At one point, the resilient Leth enthusiastically casts the action in terms of von Trier's increasingly heavy serves, and his equally determined returns. This sporting metaphor resonates with another aspect of the aesthetic debate that von Trier and Leth conduct between *#3: Brussels* and *#4: Cartoon*: von Trier speaks of the importance of the lesson he learnt from Leth concerning 'the rules of the game', that is, of establishing a set of norms or 'rules' which set the boundaries for the work of art.[3] Leth, in similar terms and in the same conversation, talks of the significance of the 'frame' adopted by a given art work, that is, the decision to explore *just this* phenomenon from *just this* point of view (the literal framing instantiated by a given film shot thus being just one example of this broader activity of framing). Once the frame and the object have been decided upon, the artist must then patiently wait for the object to reveal itself:

> I normally find places and then isolate something I want to examine. That's the method. And then I frame it very precisely and wait for the right moment. I believe very strongly in waiting and observing.

This strategy is beautifully, and explicitly, exemplified in *The Five Obstructions* in the footage documenting the shooting of *#3: Brussels*. In one of the many shots of Leth wandering through the labyrinthine corridors of the hotel in which the film is partly shot, a brief volley of lovemaking sounds catches Leth's attention. He stops and listens carefully, waiting to see if and how the sound will evolve. In fact, very little happens for the minute or so that the shot lasts; but we witness Leth watching and waiting, and we, in turn, are invited to scrutinise Leth, in this suspended state, with equal care. The shot thus not only exemplifies Leth's attachment to the long take, but displays the role of the device in his approach to film-making. And here the common ground between Leth (the aesthete) and von Trier (the romantic) – the common ground which perhaps enabled the project to be conceived at all – emerges, since both acknowledge the need for a combination of an element of control (a 'frame', a set of 'rules') and an element of chance (actors messing up, unexpected occurrences on set, unforeseen problems and opportunities).[4] The constraints imposed by the 'rules' are crucial in sharpening inventiveness: 'this is precisely the idea, and the moral, of the film – namely that restrictions and difficult decisions produce a sharpness of mind by encouraging a search for entirely new ways of proceeding.'[5] Both von Trier and Leth also seem to evince an appreciation of an implicit meta-rule: the rules can be creatively interpreted or adapted ... though what counts as a *legitimate* creative adaptation of a rule is both a vital matter, and not one on which they often converge. (Certainly the difference between exploiting a set of rules in a new way, and ignoring those rules, can be a matter of nice judgement, and may often underpin strongly contrasting evaluations of art works.) Whatever convergence there may be between von Trier and Leth, within the rules of the game they establish for *The Five Obstructions* von Trier remains resolute in his criticism of Leth throughout the film. We might then ask: who ultimately wins the game, this contest between aesthetic sensibilities?

Apparently it is von Trier, for it is he who authors the fifth and final obstruction, compelling Leth to voice the narration and agree to the film appearing in his name. Von Trier wrongfoots Leth at the last by the most audacious interpretation of the rules of their game of all, turning the *record* of the game (the documentary footage of Leth making the new films, and of Leth and von Trier in discussion at various stages of the project) into its *substance*. In other words, various other strategies having failed, von Trier subjugates Leth by making Leth his (von Trier's) vehicle of expression, even as this final film is designed to appear to be the work of Leth. Von Trier's victory is attained by giving Leth almost no scope for invention and expression: from Leth's point of view, the final obstruction amounts to 'all rules and no play' — all he gets to do is read the voice-over under von Trier's 'hawk-eared' direction. And from the outset, von Trier sets himself up as the dominant player in this game — he initiates the contest, he proposes the overall framework, and he gets to stipulate the particular constraints for each remake of *The Perfect Human*. It is, however, a rather Pyrrhic victory for von Trier; if you *compel* someone to do something, then you can hardly claim that they have come to do that thing of their own volition. (If I threaten to kill myself if you don't declare your love for me, I have reason to wonder about the sincerity of your declaration of love.) And perhaps more profoundly, *The Five Obstructions* ends up giving such salience to its formal and stylistic properties that it embodies the values of the detached, formalist aesthete as much as anything. Is it in fact Jørgen Leth who triumphs, against all the odds?

The Five Obstructions takes the form of a theme with variations — the original version of *The Perfect Human*, along with the five remakes — interleaved with sequences narrating and contextualising the project as a whole. It is this 'theme-and-variations' structure that bestows on the film its strongly — if not decisively — formalist character. David Bordwell has proposed the term *parametric* for films which make the systematic attention to and variation of style a primary focus (a 'parameter' being any dimension of style — shot scale, editing rhythm, film score, for example — which can be systematically varied).[6] One of the enabling conditions for such parametric form, according to Bordwell, is 'banality' of theme. Naturally this has been one of the more controversial aspects of a controversial idea, given that Bordwell's prime examples include directors like Yasujiro Ozu and Robert Bresson, directors celebrated by humanist critics for their profound engagement with the commitments of family life and human spirituality. Much of the sting is taken out of Bordwell's claim if we think in terms of *familiarity* rather than banality, however; it is not that Ozu's subtle explorations of family dynamics lack weight or insight, but rather that we readily recognise the dramatic terrain on which they take place. Now, *The Five Obstructions* concerns itself with something much more esoteric: the nature of art. But the form of the film creates familiarity with this theme and with the elements through which it articulates the theme, by virtue of repetition — repetition of the basic premise of *The*

Perfect Human, repetition of various motifs from the original film, and repetition of new motifs established in the new versions 'commissioned' for *The Five Obstructions*.

Why is such a high degree of familiarity (Bordwell's 'banality') necessary for parametric or 'style-centred' films? We tend to recall the 'gist' of films rather than their concrete, moment-by-moment realisation (see Bordwell 2008: 137). As a consequence, films must use special strategies to get us to notice and recall details and patterns of style. Familiarity-through-repetition is the first step in one such strategy. Against this backdrop, the distinctive style and approach of each new take on *The Perfect Human* is foregrounded. We thus move from the jazzy, jump-cut rhythms and colour splashes of *#1: Cuba*, through the deadpan cool of *#2: Bombay*, onto the arch tone and ennui-laden voice-over of *#3: Brussels*, through the psychedelic excursion that is *#4: Cartoon*, and onto the visual directness of *#5: Avedøre*. Throughout, we are reminded of the minimal, 'abstract' style of the original film which is parcelled out in increments dispersed across *The Five Obstructions*. As a group, the individual films hold together on the model of family resemblance – certain pairings contrast more strongly than others, but even the most divergent share a number of motifs. The style of each film is thus quite distinct, and the style of each film contrasts not only with the others but also with the relatively low-resolution, hand-held documentary footage that acts as the visual baseline of *The Five Obstructions*. This is true even of the sixth version; although *#5: Avedøre* is largely comprised of documentary footage shot for *The Five Obstructions*, the audacious reflexivity of the film plays up its formal dimensions in a different way. For the most part, *#5: Avedøre* relies on footage we have already seen, but now defamiliarised in black and white, and recast as the subject matter of another version of *The Perfect Human*, rather than as commentary on it.

We can best appreciate the stylistic variations on the original enacted by each of the five remakes by both considering the various 'parameters' of style that are varied, and by tracking some of the particular motifs that recur across two or more of the films.

Shot-length and compositional style vary considerably over the six films, from the long takes characteristic of the original and *#2: Bombay*,

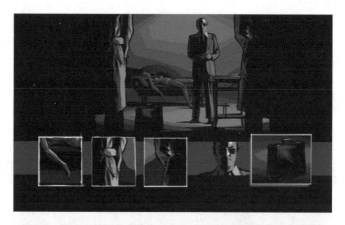

Internal frames in *#4: Cartoon*

through the intermediate shot lengths of *#3: Brussels*, to the staccato editing of *#1: Cuba*. The rapid rhythms of *#1: Cuba* reappear in *#4: Cartoon*, this time achieved through a combination of editing and intrashot animation, often taking the form of the appearance of frames-within-the-frame. Multiple internal frames are also a feature of *#3: Brussels*, but where *#4: Cartoon* moves quickly through numerous variations on this visual idea, *#3: Brussels* alternates between traditional full-frame shots and bifurcated shots, in which two spaces are juxtaposed within the larger frame (see page 129).

The *mise-en-scène* in the films varies from the abstract backdrop of the original, through the cityscapes of *#1: Cuba* and *#3: Brussels*, veering off in one direction towards the shifting, plastic world of *#4: Cartoon*, and in another direction towards the real locations revealed in the camcorder footage comprising *#5: Avedøre*. Titles aside, *The Perfect Human* is devoid of written text, but *#1: Cuba* introduces a number of bright, hand-painted intertitles. Fragments of text make fleeting appearances in *#3: Brussels* (the air ticket to Caracas) and in *#5: Avedøre* (Leth's production notes), but the textual motif is picked up with a vengeance in *#4: Cartoon*, which characteristically employs a whole variety of typefaces

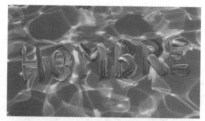

Varieties of text in *#1: Cuba* and *#4: Cartoon*

The opening shot of #2: Bombay

in different ways. (#4: *Cartoon* in general recapitulates in microcosm the parametric aspects of *The Five Obstructions*, working through numerous variations on motifs within its own boundaries.) The translucent screen introduced in #2: *Bombay*, at once separating and connecting the reality of Bombay's red light district with the artificial bubble created by

The Eurostar in #3: *Brussels*

Leth in its midst, finds an echoing motif in *#3: Brussels*. In the second shot of this film we see the Eurostar through a fence, its fuzzy presence in the foreground of the shot softening the image of the train. Later in the film, after the female character has delivered a monologue through the open window of a Mercedes, the window is electrically closed; and a few seconds later we see the male protagonist in his hotel room through a balcony window. These two partially transparent windows present us with both objects seen in reflection *on* the glass as well as the major figures seen *through* the glass.

Figure movement and gesture – what we could simply refer to as 'performance' were it not for *#5: Avedøre*, with its dependence on non-fiction footage – tend towards the stylised, although here again there are notable departures from this norm. Unsurprisingly, a more naturalistic form of gesture and movement is visible in *#5: Avedøre* than in any of the other versions, while *#2: Bombay* contrasts Leth's slow, laboured rendition of the male role, with the patient curiosity of Indian onlookers, who view Leth's antics without a trace of surprise. *#4: Cartoon*, while sustaining the generally stylised form of figure movement and gesture, adds a further level to this stylisation by evoking genre iconography – Claus Nissen's embodiment of the man in black tie is transformed here into a *film noir* icon, raincoat and cigarette displacing pipe and tuxedo.

There are also important shifts in music and sound design across the films. The original establishes a combination of voice-over (parodying the tone and register of a scientific documentary – Leth characterises the film as 'pseudo-anthropological'[7]), classical score and monologues delivered by the male character. *#1: Cuba* dispenses with the monologues and uses a jazz rather than classical score; *#2: Bombay* puts most of its weight on Leth's rendition of monologue, with a brief injection of a new classical score; *#3: Brussels* retains the emphasis on the monologue, while also fusing the monologue with the voice-over, Patrick Bauchau's voice filling both roles. The film gives greater prominence to the ambient sounds of some of the objects and locations that we see (the Eurostar train, the hotel lobby), though it also utilises a few fragments of the original classical score. *#4: Cartoon*, while retaining these three core elements, weaves together a collage of sonic fragments (including parts of the original score), in line with its visual imagery. *#5: Avedøre* brings us back to the combination of voice-over and (the original) classical score, but now the voice-over takes the form of a highly personal letter, in contrast to the detached and parodic form of the original voice-over.

Three motifs that appear in most of the versions are smoking, shaving and falling. The original film begins with Claus Nissen preparing a pipe for smoking. In a continuous long take, he is shown head on, and then in left and right profile, stroking his face pensively with the pipe before lighting up; all of these gestures and movements have a mechanical quality. *#1: Cuba* commences its virtuoso deployment of shots less than a second in length by presenting its Cuban male protagonist in a similar series of poses, but this time preparing and smoking a cigar rather than a pipe (we are, after all, in Havana). (Later, in *#4: Cartoon*, the cigar is replaced by a cigarette, the voice-over commenting on the change; the pipe never reappears, apparently deserted in the 1960s.) The movements here have a much more naturalistic character, and Leth works within the 12-frame limitation to create an unpredictable musicality in contrast to the stiff formality of the original sequence. The business of the unwrapping and lighting of the cigar takes on a choreographed form, echoed later in

The smoking motif

The shaving motif

the film by the man's Latin dance moves; here Leth edits together shots in forward and reverse motion, overcoming the 12-frame limitation to create the impression of smooth, sinuous motion. All of these movements are gathered up and animated by the jazz score. A brief shot in the original version of the woman posing with a cigar is recalled by the woman in *#3: Brussels*, who actively smokes a cigarette.

The shaving motif appears in all six films, and is most strikingly transformed in *#4: Cartoon*, where the visual treatments of the original footage flatten and distort the realistic textures of photography, so that the depiction of Leth intermittently takes on the look of a Cubist portrait (see also page 124). As for the falling motif, the male protagonists of *#1: Cuba* and *#3: Brussels* escape this indignity (Bauchau's imposing sang-froid would not have sat easily with this action), but otherwise it appears in all other versions. And very importantly, the image of Leth himself performing this action closes *#5:Avedøre* – as well as *The Five Obstructions* itself.

The Five Obstructions, then, moves in an open-ended fashion through a series of permutations on *The Perfect Human*, each new version not only adopting a different stylistic approach, but also focusing upon or developing a different aspect of the original film. Thus *#1: Cuba* restages roughly the first half of *The Perfect Human* (the smoking, dancing, eye, ear and bed sequences of the original), while *#2: Bombay* concerns itself exclusively with the second half (the meal, shaving and 'clicking fingers' sequences). *#3: Brussels* begins with the section of monologue that concludes both the original and *#2: Bombay*, proceeding to dwell upon and make explicit the erotic potential of the original – a potential which, if anything, is deliberately neutralised in the original film.

In certain respects there is a 'direction' to the variations on *The Perfect Human* enacted by *The Five Obstructions*. Generally speaking, there is an increasing density to each new version, beginning with Leth's minimal original, culminating in the multilayered *#4: Cartoon*, and easing slightly with the busily edited *#5:Avedøre*. (*#2: Bombay* is, to be sure, an exception to this rule; but if *The Five Obstructions* teaches us anything, it is that rules will rarely be followed slavishly in the domain of art.) In part this density is due to the incorporation of ideas drawn from Leth's subsequent life – the casting of Patrick Bauchau in *#3: Brussels*, for example, inspired by Leth's admiration for his performance as the protagonist of Eric Rohmer's *La collectionneuse*. Intriguingly, Rohmer's film was, like *The Perfect Human*, released in 1967; it as if Leth has chosen a better-known counterpart to Claus Nissen – an equally handsome actor from the same generation, both born in 1938 – in order to stress the effects of time and experience on the model-like 'perfection' of the figures in his original film (Leth notes the importance of Bauchau's 'well-bruised' quality to his casting in *#3: Brussels*).

More generally, all of the new versions bear the marks of Leth's career as a documentary filmmaker, an interest evident in *The Perfect Human* in only the most tangential way (in the form of the parodic voice-over,

Echoes of the city symphony: Havana in #1: Cuba

adopting a tone somewhere between the scientific documentary and the instructional film).[8] This is particularly true of *#1: Cuba* and *#3: Brussels*, both of which evoke the tradition of the city symphony. Both films throw the windows open, filling the airless white abyss of the original with the sights and sounds of the cities in which they were made; to a more limited

The riverboat in #3: Brussels

extent this is also true of *#2: Bombay*, in which Leth's meal is set against the brightly-coloured backdrop, and the humming ambience, of Falkland Road (the red light district). Towards its conclusion, *#3: Brussels* also drops in a shot from the bow of a boat travelling up a tropical river, a shot with almost surreal force in the context of this film, a sudden splash of exotic green following the sterile hotel and grey industrial tones of Brussels. Even the heavily-stylised *#4: Cartoon* is permeated by what we recognise as (now visually manipulated) documentary footage. As with the casting of Bauchau, far from simply removing us from life – to recall Hanson's characterisation of the aesthete's impulse – this seems to open the door to the 'imperfect' disarray of reality. One might argue that the aesthetic sensibility still wins out here, capturing fragments of reality but then abstracting and recontextualising them, as with the shot of the tropical river; or, most 'provocatively' of all, allowing us to glimpse Falkland Road, but only as a beautiful backdrop, a tableaux of vibrant saris (see page 126), combined with a pointed refusal to engage with the 'social drama' of poverty and prostitution.[9] Art ventures more closely towards Life, only to steal and preserve more of it on its own amoral terms, 'removed … from the strictures and obligations that properly bind us'.[10] But perhaps in venturing so close, some of the chaos and commitments of Life penetrate the work of art. If this is correct, it suggests that von Trier's charge that Leth continues to cling to an aesthetic of formal beauty is unfair.

Other ideas incorporated into the new versions are drawn from the immediate context of the dialogues with von Trier over the *The Five Obstructions*: prior to *#4: Cartoon*, for example, von Trier savours the idea of posing a set of limitations that will make Leth as helpless and vulnerable as a tortoise on its back. He believes he has found just such a scenario by ruling that the next film must take the form of a cartoon. In the film that constitutes Leth's devastating reply to von Trier, a tortoise is included among the dense network of motifs – notably, however, the tortoise is not shown flailing on its back, but rather marching steadily across the screen. Leth's patient method has indeed found another telling and unexpected solution.

Two other trends across the new versions are worth noting. While the original *The Perfect Human* is hardly a conventional narrative, it does stick

The tortoise in *#4: Cartoon*

with two characters and presents them in a series of activities, puzzling and symbolically laden as these elements may be. As the films progress, there is a subtle shift of emphasis away from narrative and towards a more lyrical quality: the visual imagery and voice-over commentary tend to spark – and hang together by virtue of – loosely related associations rather than specified narrative connections. Similarly, the final two films – *#4: Cartoon* and *#5: Avedøre* – exploit the possibilities of collage in a way that is either absent or only marginally present in the earlier versions. *#5: Avedøre* depends on the principle of collage in the sense that it creates a new object out of the fragments of a pre-existing object (that is, footage shot for, and much of it edited into, the documentary sequences of *The Five Obstructions*). Both of these trends reach their apogee in *#4: Cartoon*, a palimpsest layering material from the various 'eras' encompassed by *The Five Obstructions*, all of them then drawn upon by Bob Sabiston's animation techniques; in this film, above all, narrative sequencing is overwhelmed by intricate, concentrated audio-visual design. Leth's comments in the interview footage leading up to *#4: Cartoon* highlight the importance of collage and 're-use'. Not to be outdone, von Trier makes a parallel move by turning to collage in the final obstruction, but substituting the drabness of monochrome hand-held footage for the shifting colour schemes and strange textures of Sabiston's animation.

The final straw

The decree that Leth's fourth remake of *The Perfect Human* should take the form of a cartoon appears to be the most decisive and vicious blow aimed at Leth by von Trier. Von Trier can't stand cartoons, and he knows that animation is anathema to Leth as well. Von Trier seems to imagine that Leth will feel obliged to tackle the techniques of animation, many of which take years – as well as some degree of latent aptitude – to master. Leth will thereby be humbled and humiliated, reduced to a childlike – decidedly imperfect – grasp of his aesthetic medium. Leth makes the 'knight's move',[11] however, simply engaging a highly skilled (and fashionable) animator as a collaborator and technical assistant – just about any form of filmmaking is collaborative, so why not? No rule or limitation is broken by bringing Sabiston into play, just as no rule is broken when Leth employs those other creative collaborators known as 'performers' in *#1: Cuba* and *#3: Brussels*. The single, apparently devastating, stipulation in Obstruction #4 turns out to be von Trier's biggest gift to Leth.

Sabiston's particular style of animation is also integral to the solution that Leth finds to the problem posed by von Trier's commandment. Sabiston is perhaps best known for his feature-length collaborations with Richard Linklater, *Waking Life* (2001) and *A Scanner Darkly* (2006). The animation technique employed by Sabiston on these projects, as well as on *#4: Cartoon*, is a computer-enhanced version of rotoscoping – a form of animation which uses live-action film footage as its basis, tracing over outlines and textures to create a basic animated image, which can then be subjected to further treatments.[12] The key point for us here is that this particular animation technique is one which preserves a connection with live-action footage – and in the case of documentary footage, with that bit of the world captured by the camera and microphone. Leth thus eschews the complete 'detachment from the world' afforded by traditional animation – the creation of an alternative, infinitely plastic universe in which just about anything can happen. Von Trier and Leth's shared abhorrence of standard animation, along with the way in which Leth uses animation techniques in *#4: Cartoon*, suggest again that Leth's formalism – his commitment to 'perfection' – is not simply *opposed* to an appreciation of reality, as von Trier implies.

The extent of Leth's victory over von Trier in relation to this episode is evident from von Trier's immediate reaction after seeing *#4: Cartoon*: 'I think it's a beautiful film.' The word 'beautiful', or at least the way that von Trier uses the word here, sums up in the most succinct fashion the very concept of perfection – detached and abstracted from life – that so irks von Trier. He tries to elicit an ugly and incompetent work from Leth, the redeeming feature of which would be its embodiment of Leth's real imperfection. But Leth delivers a film whose sheer visual dynamism virtually silences von Trier. Back to the drawing board.

Jørgen Lars Leth von Trier

The game of style is a particularly salient type of interest created by *The Five Obstructions*. It is hard not to notice, and to take pleasure in, the various formal and stylistic strategies that are mined across the film – notice and take pleasure in them *for their own sake*, that is. As we have seen, however, the game of style is by no means entirely free-standing. The game also functions as a means of argument within a serious dispute about the ethics of art (as well as the nature of self-knowledge – as we will see). In other words, the game of style is tightly integrated with the narrative and dramatic structure of the film; it is the vehicle through which the two antagonists pursue their goals. In this way the film articulates a version of parametric form distinct from those discussed by Bordwell, in which the systematic variation of style occurs, as it were, in parallel with or overlaid upon the narrative structure of the film. The parametric play with *mise-en-scène* in Ozu, for example, creates a layer of design and aesthetic interest in addition and irreducible to narrative design and interest. By contrast, in *The Five Obstructions* the game of style is narrativised; the variations in style have an overt motivation in the narrative contest recounted by the film. Even so, the variations are not motivated in the traditional manner as apt stylistic expressions of theme. Instead, the drama of the film precisely

challenges the idea that style in art always and necessarily emerges organi-
cally from the needs of the subject matter. In this way *The Five Obstructions* retains the character of parametric or 'style-centred' form even as it
binds the play with style closely into its dramatic form.

The game of style is, then, the vehicle of a dramatically rendered argument about a serious matter. But there is 'serious' and there is serious. Even in respect of the themes of art and self-knowledge, the film
is exceptionally arch and self-conscious, dwelling on the jesting, playful
interactions between the two disputants, and elaborating a whole variety
of metaphorical renderings of their relationship through which the drama
is played out. The principal metaphors in play across the film include:

> master – apprentice
> therapist – patient
> master/dominatrix – submissive

It is important to note that von Trier and Leth do not consistently play the
equivalent roles in these metaphorical couplings – thus, while von Trier
mostly occupies the 'active' roles of 'therapist' and 'master/dominatrix',
Leth is, originally at least, the 'master' to von Trier's 'apprentice'. These
metaphors are explicitly put into play by von Trier and Leth in their
dialogues in the film. Two other, related metaphors are more implicit.
The first of these is the Hegelian 'master/servant' dialectic, the relevance
of which here hinges on the numerous occasions and ways in which
the apparently weaker, subordinated figure turns out to have a surprising
amount of power in a given situation. The second overarching metaphor
is given to us by the title of the film itself, which evokes the idea of religious, or at least spiritual, tests of faith and ability. *The Five Obstructions*
'conceptually blends' the implications of these various metaphors.[13]

It is not only the concepts that get blended, however. As I have hinted,
the stances of the two filmmakers may not be as sharply opposed as von
Trier wishes to believe (if only for the sake of the drama that the film
creates). This convergence or overlap – dare one say, the synthesis arising
from the thesis and antithesis – between von Trier and Leth is made concrete in *The Five Obstructions*' concluding section. Recall that, for the final

obstruction, von Trier stipulates that *he* will make the film, based on foot-age of the dialogues and the shooting of the remakes. Von Trier will also write the voice-over in the form of a letter from Leth to von Trier; and this narration will be voiced by Leth. These rules generate a final remake that is full of paradox. The conjunction of Leth's voice, speaking in the first person, uttering highly plausible sentiments, makes it easy to forget that this is von Trier's film. The text includes many passages in which von Trier has imagined what and how Leth might imagine what von Trier had to say about Leth. The effect of this triple-embedding of levels is dis-orienting. The conceit of *#5: Avedøre* makes it very difficult to keep the voices and stances of the two contestants distinct from one another.[14]

Perhaps this is not an accident. On one hand, we have seen that Leth's style – as evidenced by the remakes – is not straightforwardly guilty of von Trier's charge of 'provocative, perverse perfection'. On the other hand, much of what von Trier says of Leth might be said of von Trier himself, looking at his wider oeuvre. The emphasis on role-playing, and the adoption of a particular set of rules or conventions for a given proj-ect, but always in a playful, partly self-mocking way, are familiar motifs in von Trier's career. Just as the Dogma 95 manifesto adopts a righteous, pseudo-fundamentalist tone, so here von Trier's adoption of the role of stern but caring therapist comes across as still another guise to be adopted. This doesn't make von Trier guilty of an obsessive concern with detached, formal beauty, separated from the currents of life. But then, no one is charging him with that crime. The point, rather, is that von Trier is com-mitted, like Leth but in his own way, to an oblique and artful engagement with reality – a far cry from the raw reflection of human imperfection that he lays out as an aspiration for Leth. Von Trier recognises his artistic kinship with Leth in the voice-over for *#5: Avedøre*, in which von Trier is described as being part of the same 'family' as Leth. But the recognition is only partial, for this 'admission' comes buried within the indirect and disguised narration of this film (von Trier imagining what Leth might imagine von Trier saying of himself and of his motivations for *The Five Obstructions* project). We may be inclined to say of von Trier, however, as he says of Leth just prior to the screening of film *#5: Avedøre*, 'I think I know considerably more about him than he does.'[15]

NOTES

1   Leth has commented on the centrality of this dramatic contest to the film: 'It is important to understand that our shared assumption is that making films should be fun and exciting, preferably difficult, and never ever boring. I am aware that I am putting my professional reputation at risk, and this is in fact precisely what makes the project interesting to me. I think this is very important in terms of the kind of intensity and even suspense that eventually develops as the film unfolds. I suspect the audience is aware of the authenticity of what is happening. How evil is that von Trier capable of becoming? And how much longer will that Leth be able to come up with suitable responses to von Trier's taunts?' 'The *Dekalog* Interview: Jørgen Leth', this volume, 144–5.

2   'The *Dekalog* Interview: Jørgen Leth', this volume, 142.

3   'Both Lars and I like the idea of a game with rules – and we respect the rules.' 'The *Dekalog* Interview: Jørgen Leth', this volume, 144.

4   'The *Dekalog* Interview: Jørgen Leth', this volume, 142, 143. Leth also reflects on the role of chance in his approach to filmmaking in 'Gifts of Chance – A Poetics of Cinema', in the booklet accompanying *The Jørgen Leth Collection: The Anthropological Films* (Danish Film Institute, 2007), the first in a projected six-volume collection of Leth's film work.

5   'The *Dekalog* Interview: Jørgen Leth', this volume, 146.

6   The idea runs through many of Bordwell's works, but its most detailed and explicit formulation remains chapter 12 of *Narration in the Fiction Film* (1985). *The Five Obstructions* exemplifies the 'replete' version of parametric form, in which a film explores numerous different stylistic possibilities. Bordwell contrasts such replete form with the 'sparse' approach to style, in which a film restricts itself to an unusually narrow range of stylistic options, mining subtle variations within this narrow range.

7   'Gifts of Chance,' op.cit.

8   Testimony to the significance of the documentary dimension of Leth's films can be found in *The Anthropological Films*. Among other films, the volume includes both *The Perfect Human* and *The Five Obstructions*. Leth studied ethnography in the early 1960s, and acknowledges Bronislaw Malinowski as an important source of inspiration.

9   Leth uses the phrase 'social drama' in *The Five Obstructions*, in the interviews

shot during the preparation for #2: Bombay, to refer to the kind of situation into which von Trier wants to propel him.

10 Peter Schepelern's essay in this volume pursues this thesis in relation to The Five Obstructions, and Leth's career more generally. Schepelern writes, for example: '[Leth's] general project, it seems, is a fusion of life and work, a wholly aestheticised approach to both life and art.' 'To Calculate the Moment', 96.

11 Viktor Shklovsky's polyvalent metaphor for the oblique and unpredictable nature of artistic development; see his Knight's Move (2005). There are further intriguing parallels between Shklovsky's and Leth's aesthetic stances. Both insist upon the importance of form, the constraints imposed by form, and the creativity that such constraints drive. Shklovsky was one of the architects of twentieth-century formalism, insisting on the autonomous nature and development of art. Knight's Move is a virtual manifesto for formalism. And yet, one of the first essays in this volume is a vivid analysis of the impact of war and privation on human behaviour, 'Petersburg During the Blockade' (see 9–20). As Shklovsky argued elsewhere, the purpose of art is to defamiliarise the habitual; and the experience of war, like any experience, can become habitual. Shklovsky's position is more complex than some of his own declarations imply. For neither Shklovsky nor Leth would it be true to say that the formalist impulse excludes the ethical impulse, no matter how vital the former.

12 Sabiston christened the software that he designed, patented and uses for his animated films Rotoshop. It enables 'interpolated rotoscoping', in which two non-adjacent frames on a strip of live-action footage are hand-traced, the drawings for the intervening frames then being calculated automatically by the computer. The interpolated lines and shapes produce extremely fluid motion, creating the distinctive Rotoshop texture in which the smooth development of the interpolated frames is conjoined with the rougher-hewn quality of the hand-drawn frames. The hand-drawn frames also establish the 'template' for the particular graphic style of any given Rotoshopped sequence – a style that, as #4: Cartoon demonstrates, is open to infinite variation.

13 On conceptual blending, see Fauconnier & Turner (2002).

14 The human capacity to hold in mind embedded levels of thought or belief – my beliefs about what you believe about her beliefs, and so on – weakens notably with third- and fourth-order beliefs, becoming chronically unreliable with fifth-level tasks. See Peter Kinderman et al., 1998: 197.

15 My thanks to Mette Hjort, David Bordwell and Marit Knollmueller for helpful feedback and commentary on earlier drafts of this essay.

WORKS CITED

Bordwell, David (1985) 'Parametric Narration', in *Narration in the Fiction Film*. Madison, WI: University of Wisconsin Press, 274–310.

_____ (2008) 'Cognition and Comprehension: Viewing and Forgetting in Mildred Pierce', Poetics of Cinema. New York: Routledge, 135–50.

Fauconnier, Gilles and Mark Turner (2002) *The Way We Think: Conceptual Blending and the Mind's Hidden Complexities*. New York: Basic Books.

Hanson, Karen (1998) 'How bad can good art be?', in Jerrold Levinson (ed.) *Aesthetics and Ethics: Essays at the Intersection*. Cambridge: Cambridge University Press, 204–26.

Kinderman, Peter, Robin Dunbar and Richard P. Bentall (1998) 'Theory-of-mind deficits and causal attributions', *British Journal of Psychology*, 89, 191–204.

Leth, Jørgen (2007) 'Gifts of Chance – A Poetics of Cinema', in *The Jørgen Leth Collection: The Anthropological Films*. Copenhagen: Danish Film Institute.

Shklovsky, Viktor (2005) *Knight's Move*, trans. Richard Sheldon. Normal, IL: Dalkey Archive Press.

The *Dekalog* Interview: Jørgen Leth[1]

Mette Hjort: As is often the case with Lars von Trier's projects, *The Five Obstructions* is accompanied and framed by manifesto-style statements. Von Trier's statement foregrounds the need, in documentary works, somehow to 'defocus', whereas yours focuses on questions of flow, on fleeting moments that must be captured. Could you point to precise moments in *The Five Obstructions* that are the result of an attempt to put into practice these programmatic statements, both yours and von Trier's?

Jørgen Leth: We did not discuss manifestos or statements before or during the conversations about the individual remakes. I think we both view those kinds of statements as background knowledge, as something we carry around as baggage. We both work very intensely with experimental film language, and we both have a polemical relationship to existing norms. As a result we feel the need, every now and again, to write down the ideas we have for making films. Often this will take the form of updating our working process. New experiences can be captured in a few sentences. I have always tried, along the way, to formulate my cinematic poetics clearly and comprehensibly. And every now and again I update my practice.

I find it very inspiring to think about what I call 'the instant', the idea of time as an almost liquid substance. There are these instants that pass and they have to be captured and framed. That idea is always present in my work. However, I can't really claim to have understood Lars' concept of 'defocus'; and as far as I can tell this concept never really became part of the process of working with *The Five Obstructions*. On the other hand, he did immediately target my preference for long takes in the first remake, the one that was shot in Havana. When he asked me to work with only 12 frames per take he was going against my inclination to work with long takes, in which time is allowed to pass and where there is room for observation and immersion.

MH: Von Trier's attempt throughout is to get you to 'produce some real shit' ('lave noget lort'), which he defines at one point as something that hasn't been fully planned and executed. Your stance as a filmmaker has never, however, involved attempts at total mastery, for you have always made a point of making room for the magical participation of chance. How do you make sense of von Trier's obsession, in *The Five Obstructions*, with this idea of artistic garbage or shit?

JL: Well he understands what I am doing, and what I feel like doing. He is a kind of expert in my work and credits me with having influenced his own work through my films. He knows that I like to work in a place that lies somewhere between constraint and freedom. He knows that I often wish to let go and lose control in the middle of a film shoot. That is part of my practice. I like to see what happens when I do that sort of thing, when I invite chance to play a role in the process. I think that attitude presents a challenge for him. He himself is, of course, a kind of control freak. But he does like to play. For me openness towards chance occurrences is something that can be used quite naturally in the creative process.

MH: All of the nested *The Perfect Human* versions or 'remakes' are about five minutes long. Was there a length constraint on which the two directors of *The Five Obstructions* had agreed in advance?

ON THE FIVE OBSTRUCTIONS

JL: Yes, that was something we had reached an agreement about in our original correspondence about the project.

MH: Are the embedded 'obstruction' films presented in their entirety?

JL: Yes, they have all been made to measure, so to speak. We didn't make any films that were longer or in any way different from what you see in *The Five Obstructions*. The idea was to have the remakes focus on selected scenes from the original film, the scene with the meal, for example.

MH: How much collaboration, between you and von Trier, was there in the making of the embedded films?

JL: Lars would express his wishes and propose things during our conversations. It was clear from the outset that this was where he wished to put his mark on the collaborative process. He didn't want to be part of the process of actually making the individual films, or to be part of the editing. Not even in the last remake, which he of course wrote. This particular division of labour was never really discussed. It was self-evident to both of us from the very outset.

MH: The credits list Camilla Skousen and Morten Højbjerg as the editors of the film. Does that include the editing of the remakes of *The Perfect Human*? Who did the editing of *The Perfect Human: Cuba*, for example?

JL: Yes, they edited the entire film and all of its elements, that is, both the individual remakes and all the material from the conversations and shooting situations. Camilla and Morten are 'my' people. Camilla has edited all my films since 1985, and she knows what I like; she has an intuitive grasp of the direction in which I want the film to go. This is absolutely crucial, as I never work with a script that arranges scenes in a certain sequence. And in recent years I have often been in Haiti while Camilla was doing the editing in Denmark. She suggested Morten as co-editor; he was her student at the National Film School of Denmark, and has now embarked on a very promising career himself.

143

MH: One of the film's nice features is its marvellous, improvised quality: one really has the impression of being a fly on the wall watching completely spontaneous, unedited encounters between von Trier and yourself. How accurate or inaccurate is this impression? Did you, for example, make several takes of any of the 'Leth encounters von Trier' sequences? Was the editing of such sequences supervised by both of you?

JL: The conversations are exactly as spontaneous as they look. There isn't a single extra take that didn't make it into the final film. We never prepared what we were going to talk about, and never agreed in advance on the general direction of our conversations. These were all conversations that developed quite naturally, although at times with rather surprising leaps. I never had any idea what he might think of next. And this was, of course, precisely the feature of the situation that made it all exciting for us both. I reacted to what he said and proposed suggestions, and it was clear that the idea of somehow changing these exchanges was absolutely out of the question. We never modified what was said or manipulated what the two cameras recorded. Both Lars and I like the idea of a game with rules – and we respect the rules. It was also unthinkable that we might meet after the individual exchanges and discuss the topics that had come up, the contents of the exchanges, for example, and the way they had unfolded. If we did meet – there was, for example, a dinner in a top restaurant outside of Copenhagen after the very tough discussion of the Bombay remake – we would talk in a very relaxed and amicable way about completely different things.

I repeat: the idea that we might later reconsider the decisions that we made or the agreements we reached was unthinkable. Everything is in the film. Nothing has been left out. It is important to understand that our shared assumption is that making films should be fun and exciting, preferably difficult, and never ever boring. I am aware that I am putting my professional reputation at risk, and this is in fact precisely what makes the project interesting to me. I think this is very important in terms of the kind of intensity and even suspense that eventually develops as the film unfolds. I suspect the audience is aware of the authenticity of what is happening. How evil is that von Trier capable of becoming? And how much longer will that Leth be able to come up with suitable responses to von Trier's taunts?

MH: The DVD includes poems, written by you, in an attempt to capture the essence of your meetings. How, more prosaically, would you describe these meetings?

JL: I prefer to let things stand the way they are registered in the film. My poems attempt to express what was happening, what the set-up for our meetings was, and what the mood was like.

MH: The DVD includes a so-called 'alternative ending'. What, for you, are the key differences between this ending and the fifth obstruction that concludes the film? Was the decision to make this alternative ending and include it in the DVD options a collaborative one?

JL: I don't actually remember the details here. It's been a very long time since I've seen the alternative ending. We dropped it because we felt the other one was better.

MH: Both endings show images of a deeply moved and emotional Leth. Why were you so close to tears in these scenes?

JL: Quite simply because the words that Lars wrote and had me say really touched me. I felt that he was really pushing things, much more so than on any of the other occasions, in terms of his self-knowledge, his description of his own ambitions for the film, and his recognition of the resistance he encountered. He almost gives me too much credit. I was just deeply moved by the generosity that he expressed in that epilogue.

MH: Who controlled the budget and shooting schedule for each of the obstructions? Was it von Trier, or some Zentropa producer(s), who determined how much could be spent on each of the films? Was the budget established for *The Five Obstructions* project as a whole, with someone (von Trier?) deciding on a more or less case-by-case basis how much money and time to allot to a given obstruction? Did you or your production company contribute any financing to *The Five Obstructions* at any phase of the project, from pre- to post-production?

JL: My company, Sunset Productions, only participated to a limited extent in the financing. The money came from the Danish Film Institute and from foreign co-production partners. Zentropa Real producer Carsten Holst determined the budget for each section of the film. He was quite tough. My producer, Marianne Christensen, then fought hard to get the best possible conditions for us during shooting; she knows my luxury habits. She got Zentropa to understand that I work best under optimal conditions. Good hotels, decent meals, and that kind of thing. Lars didn't want to interfere with the production details, but it was of course clear from the outset that he wanted a certain extravagance at the level of production, in the form of distant locations, for example. His attitude was also reflected in the premise (never discussed) that all remakes would be shot on film. When he, towards the end of the first conversation, asks Carsten Holst, who is outside the room, whether there might be enough money to send me and my (expensive) crew to Cuba, it's really more an order than a question. It is after all Lars who, together with Peter Aalbæk, calls the shots at Zentropa. In short, we lived well, but we also had a very tight budget for the actual film. And this is actually how I prefer to work. We could only shoot a very limited number of metres of film. This sharpened our inventiveness, not least in the Havana sequence where we constantly had to move the camera around while shooting the individual scenes, in order to ensure that we would have as many different editing options as possible. But this is precisely the idea, and the moral, of the film – namely that restrictions and difficult decisions produce a sharpness of mind by encouraging a search for entirely new ways of proceeding.

MH: In *The Five Obstructions* neither you nor von Trier make any but the most oblique, implicit references to budgetary matters (for example when you mention the impossibility of certain strategies of response to the cartoon obstruction). Why is this financial dimension of the very expensive game that you are playing occluded to such a degree? As presented to viewers, *The Five Obstructions* makes it look as if the game was conducted in a financial vacuum, with neither player having to worry about cash flow, completion bonds, contingency funds, expense reports, profit margins, advances on distribution, and so on. But in terms of games, film-making is more Monopoly than it is 'truth or dare'.

JL: I think it is because we both celebrate the idea that small budgets are good budgets. I always want a budget that limits my technical possibilities. It is, of course, quite satisfying when experienced people first tell you that it's impossible to realise the idea of an animated sequence, and you then meet Bob Sabiston who, without any problems whatsoever, meets the challenge in the most innovative way, within the constraints of the budget, and in record time! I also feel much freer when working with my 'exclusive' experimental approach to making films, if I am not up against huge expectations from a large general audience. I am used to a small but very faithful audience. I like the thought that I can afford to experiment. The legitimacy of my films cannot be found at the box office.

MH: When you were working on *The Five Obstructions* did you think of it as a work of fiction or non-fiction (and, if so, in what sense)? Or was such a classification simply not pertinent?

JL: We are, of course, working exactly on the border between fiction and non-fiction. This is a terrain (we might even call it a *terrain vague*) that I have always been interested in exploring, and I have done this in various ways in a number of very different films. This perspective blurs the distinction, but it does not of course cancel the invitation that is present throughout the film to experience precisely this balancing act between fantasy and fact.

NOTE

1   This interview was conducted, in Danish, by Mette Hjort in the summer of 2006. Two of the questions were provided by Paisley Livingston and Trevor Ponech.

The *Dekalog* Re-View

Each issue of *Dekalog* will also include a 'Re-View' section where readers' feedback will be edited by respective guest editors and published in subsequent editions.

All readers are therefore very much invited to participate in the discussions, or raise issues for debate as instigated by any of the contributions to the volumes in this series, by contacting any of the series' guest editors on the following email address: dekalog@wallflowerpress.co.uk

Thank you.